I0050569

TAJIKISTAN TRANSPORT SECTOR ASSESSMENT

DECEMBER 2021

ASIAN DEVELOPMENT BANK

ADB

Creative Commons Attribution 3.0 IGO license (CC BY 3.0 IGO)

© 2021 Asian Development Bank
6 ADB Avenue, Mandaluyong City, 1550 Metro Manila, Philippines
Tel +63 2 8632 4444; Fax +63 2 8636 2444
www.adb.org

Some rights reserved. Published in 2021.

ISBN 978-92-9269-214-8 (print); 978-92-9269-215-5 (electronic); 978-92-9269-216-2 (ebook)
Publication Stock No. TCS210478-2
DOI: http://dx.doi.org/10.22617/TCS210478-2

The views expressed in this publication are those of the authors and do not necessarily reflect the views and policies of the Asian Development Bank (ADB) or its Board of Governors or the governments they represent.

ADB does not guarantee the accuracy of the data included in this publication and accepts no responsibility for any consequence of their use. The mention of specific companies or products of manufacturers does not imply that they are endorsed or recommended by ADB in preference to others of a similar nature that are not mentioned.

By making any designation of or reference to a particular territory or geographic area, or by using the term "country" in this document, ADB does not intend to make any judgments as to the legal or other status of any territory or area.

This work is available under the Creative Commons Attribution 3.0 IGO license (CC BY 3.0 IGO) https://creativecommons.org/licenses/by/3.0/igo/. By using the content of this publication, you agree to be bound by the terms of this license. For attribution, translations, adaptations, and permissions, please read the provisions and terms of use at https://www.adb.org/terms-use#openaccess.

This CC license does not apply to non-ADB copyright materials in this publication. If the material is attributed to another source, please contact the copyright owner or publisher of that source for permission to reproduce it. ADB cannot be held liable for any claims that arise as a result of your use of the material.

Please contact pubsmarketing@adb.org if you have questions or comments with respect to content, or if you wish to obtain copyright permission for your intended use that does not fall within these terms, or for permission to use the ADB logo.

Corrigenda to ADB publications may be found at http://www.adb.org/publications/corrigenda.

Notes:
In this publication, "$" refers to United States dollars.

ADB recognizes "China" as the People's Republic of China and "Kyrgyz" as the Kyrgyz Republic.

On the cover: Tajikistan plays an essential role for ensuring connectivity and facilitating movement of goods and people in the region, despite its mountainous terrains and severe climate conditions.

Cover design by Rocilyn L. Laccay.

Contents

Tables, Figures, and Maps

Figures

Maps

Acknowledgments

This report was prepared by Rika Idei, transport specialist, Transport and Communications Division (CWTC), Central and West Asia Department (CWRD), Asian Development Bank; Farrukh Nuriddinov, senior project officer, Tajikistan Resident Mission (TJRM); and Serge Cartier and Shuhrat Nurubloev, consultants. The consultants contributed greatly to collecting a wide range of data and information and compiling these in the report with detailed analysis. When finalizing the report, the team received additional support from Professor Hironori Kato, University of Tokyo, Japan. Maria Cecilia Villanueva (project analyst, CWTC), Wendy Nazal Montealto (senior operations assistant, CWTC), Mufara Hamidova (senior project assistant, TJRM), and Firuz Safarov (project assistant, TJRM) provided administrative support. The team was supervised and guided by CWRD management.

The team's great appreciation extends to government agencies in Tajikistan for providing data and information and engaging in discussions during report preparation.

The team wishes to thank the peer reviewers in CWTC and TJRM, the Sustainable Development and Climate Change Department (Transport Sector and Governance Thematic Groups), and the Independent Evaluation Department for their valuable comments.

Abbreviations

ADB	Asian Development Bank
BCP	border crossing point
CAA	Civil Aviation Agency
CAREC	Central Asia Regional Economic Cooperation
COVID-19	coronavirus disease
EBRD	European Bank for Reconstruction and Development
GBAO	Gorno–Badakhshan Autonomous Oblast
GDP	gross domestic product
GUSAD	Government Automobile Road Establishment
km	kilometer
km/h	kilometer per hour
m	meter
MOT	Ministry of Transport
NTDPTS	National Target Development Program for the Transport Sector of the Republic of Tajikistan up to 2025
OJSC	open joint-stock company
PRC	People's Republic of China
RAMS	road asset management system
SUE	state unitary enterprise
SWD	speed with delays

1. Introduction

1.   Tajikistan is a landlocked and mountainous country in Central Asia surrounded by Afghanistan,[1] the People's Republic of China (PRC), the Kyrgyz Republic, and Uzbekistan. About 93% of Tajikistan's terrain is mountainous,[2] complicating transport and transit. Most of the transport infrastructure was built during the Soviet period and was designed to optimize the Soviet system of interrepublic linkages. After the independence in 1991, relationships between Tajikistan and the neighboring countries changed and the Tajik Civil War erupted, affecting the transport networks and eventually reducing intercountry transport traffic volumes and trades. As per the National Target Development Program for the Transport Sector of the Republic of Tajikistan up to 2025 (NTDPTS),[3] the passenger transport was reduced by three-quarters, the freight transport by two-thirds, and the freight turnover by three-quarters during 1990–1996. Consequently, the transport sector funding was also significantly reduced, resulting in a severe deterioration of the transport infrastructure due to lack of maintenance.

2.   The country depends heavily on its road network to support and promote its economic activities and facilitate international trade with the neighboring countries and beyond. The limited availability of the railway infrastructure has motivated freight traders and travelers to use road transport more. The role of rail and air transport is now largely limited to international transport, primarily to Kazakhstan, the Russian Federation, and Uzbekistan. Tajikistan's ailing transport infrastructure and geographic isolation lead to high transport costs and limited access to markets and services, constraining the country's further development. In 2019, Tajikistan's gross domestic product (GDP) per capita was $890.54 and the poverty rate was 26.3%.[4] More poor people tend to live in rural areas where transport networks are underdeveloped.[5]

3.   Tajikistan's transport networks and systems must be redefined as to their roles in the country and the Central Asia region by reflecting newly emerging needs and changed relations with the neighboring countries. Such strategic approaches would help augment the roles of the transport sector infrastructure to boost the country's growth.

4.   Tajikistan has achieved constant economic growth, evidenced by the increase in the GDP from $6.5 billion in 2011 to $8.2 billion in 2020 and the average growth rate of 6.9%.[6] One driver underlying this achievement is the development of transport infrastructure, which was accomplished with assistance from development partners.

---

[1]   ADB placed on hold its assistance in Afghanistan effective 15 August 2021. https://www.adb.org/news/adb-statement-afghanistan (Published on: 10 November 2021).

[2]   United Nations Development Programme. Climate Change Adaptation. Tajikistan. https://www.adaptation-undp.org/explore/central-asia/tajikistan.

[3]   Government of Tajikistan. 2011. *National Target Development Program for the Transport Sector of the Republic of Tajikistan up to 2025*. Decree No. 165. Dushanbe.

[4]   *World Bank*. World Bank Open Data: GDP per capita (current US$) of Tajikistan (accessed 20 October 2021); and World Bank. Poverty in Tajikistan 2020 (accessed 20 October 2021). Poverty rate here is defined as a rate of populations who live below the national poverty lines against the total population.

[5]   The poverty rate in Tajikistan's rural areas was 30.2% in 2019, compared with 18.4% in the urban area (footnote 4).

[6]   World Bank. World Bank Open Data: GDP (current US$) of Tajikistan (accessed 20 October 2021); and GDP growth (annual %) of Tajikistan (accessed 20 October 2021).

5.   Cognizant of the fundamental importance of the transport sector for Tajikistan's further growth, the Asian Development Bank (ADB) carried out this transport sector assessment to review the status of the transport sector and identify issues for the sector's future development. The assessment was developed primarily through consultations with the Ministry of Transport (MOT), which leads the sector, each subsector's relevant agencies, and development partners working in the transport sector. The assessment has been prepared as a living document. It provides the recent status of the country's transport sector and its subsectors including roads, railways, civil aviation, and cross-border facilities. It also identifies major issues and challenges together with the corresponding proposals for the sector's future operation.

6.   The assessment builds on prior initiatives. In 2011, ADB helped the government develop the transport sector master plan[7] based on which the government finalized and approved the NTDPTS.

---

[7]   ADB. 2011. *Developing Tajikistan's Transport Sector: Transport Sector Master Plan.* Manila.

2. Sector Policy Framework

7.	Tajikistan's transport sector is governed by several national strategies including the National Development Strategy of the Republic of Tajikistan for the Period up to 2030,[8] the Medium-Term Development Program 2016–2020,[9] and the NTDPTS (footnote 3). Institutionally, the transport sector is managed by the MOT, together with various agencies, enterprises, and institutions.

2.1 Government Strategy

8.	The National Development Strategy of the Republic of Tajikistan for the Period up to 2030 aims to foster an independent, prosperous, and stable environment for the country's growth. One of the four strategic development objectives is to change the country from a transport dead end to a transit hub, following the National Development Plan 2000–2015, by improving transport infrastructure, developing transit corridors, and enhancing the interregional and intra-regional connectivity through multimodal development. Specifically relating to the transport sector, the strategy mentions the need to (i) develop local airports to provide affordable air transport to all regions, (ii) connect all regions by paved roads that are accessible year-round, and (iii) develop logistics centers throughout the country. Freight turnover is expected to double from 6.3 billion ton-kilometers (km) in 2015 to 12.3 billion ton-km in 2030. Passenger transport is also expected to double from 10.6 billion passenger-km to 20.6 billion passenger-km in the same period. The modality of public–private partnerships is proposed to boost financial resources.

9.	The Medium-Term Development Program 2016–2020 emphasizes the need to improve transport infrastructure linking the different areas of Tajikistan and connecting it to neighboring countries. The program identifies as critical problems the road network's poor condition; limited railway connectivity with neighboring countries; insufficient air services throughout Tajikistan; and the absence of logistics centers, resulting in low transit potential and poor access to seaports. It thus prioritizes developing transport corridors (roads, railways, and air) and their associated infrastructure linking to different countries, including logistics centers and border terminals. It also aims to increase budget allocations for road maintenance and improving data availability and databases. A new medium-term development program for 2021–2026 is under preparation by the government.

10.	In 2011, the NTDPTS was adopted as the primary guiding document for the transport sector (footnote 3). This 15-year sector program is built on these policy goals: minimizing total transport costs, focusing on developing each transport mode where it has the highest benefits, augmenting the transit and tourism potential of Tajikistan, and ensuring free competition between transport operators. Given that most of Tajikistan's geography is mountainous, road transport is the main transport means for goods and people within the country and the neighboring countries. Railway transport is the largest carrier of international transportation of goods and

---

[8]	Government of Tajikistan. 2017. *National Development Strategy of the Republic of Tajikistan for the Period up to 2030.* Dushanbe.

[9]	Government of Tajikistan, Ministry of Economic Development and Trade. 2016. *Mid-Term Development Programme of the Republic of Tajikistan for 2016–2020.* Dushanbe.

people. The civil aviation subsector is also expected to be strengthened through the operational reform and the improvement of airports and associated facilities, which would help augment the country's transit and tourism potential and promote the competitiveness of the national airlines in the markets.

11.   Road infrastructure development has currently been financed through loans and grants from development partners. These loans and grants are suggested to be replaced with road user charges or private sector financing. The importance of local authorities' participation in managing local roads in their regions is also acknowledged. Rail transport is to be self-financing for developing the existing infrastructure using its revenues and mobilizing private sector capital. The self-financing operation of air transport is also pursued improving airports, terminals, and air traffic control and attracting more private resources.

2.2 Institutional Framework

12.   The transport sector is managed by the MOT, which has seven departments with 111 staff (77 professional and 34 support staff) (Figure 1).

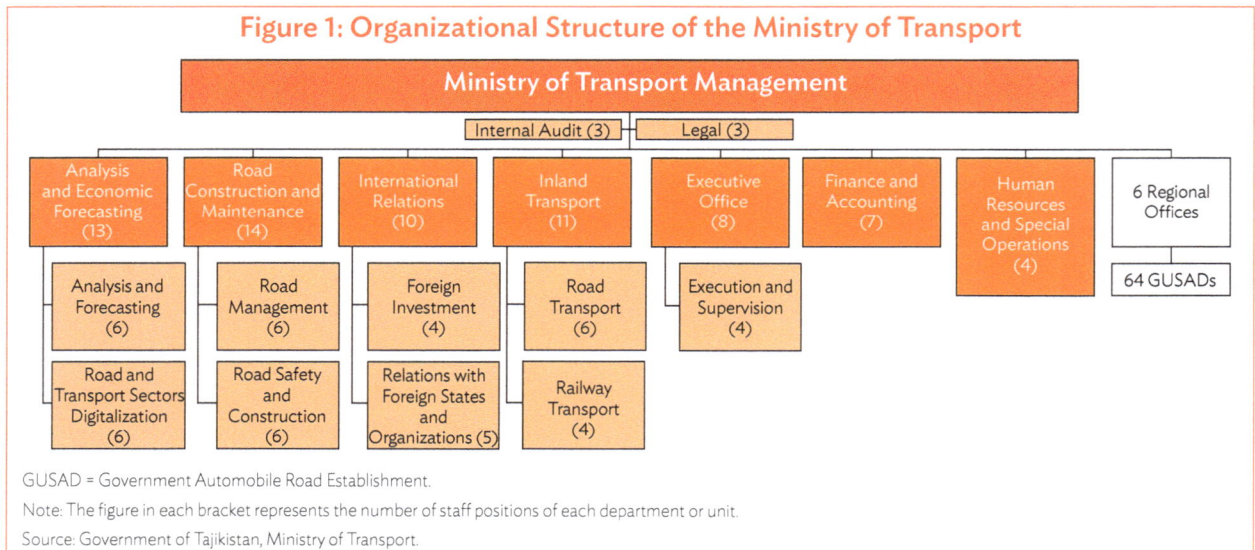

Figure 1: Organizational Structure of the Ministry of Transport

GUSAD = Government Automobile Road Establishment.

Note: The figure in each bracket represents the number of staff positions of each department or unit.

Source: Government of Tajikistan, Ministry of Transport.

13.   As shown in Figure 2, there are several open joint-stock companies (OJSCs), state institutes, and state unitary enterprises (SUEs) under the MOT that are involved in the different transport subsectors for operation and management. In addition, there are state-owned enterprises including Tajikistan Railways, Tajik Air, and Dushanbe International Airport, through which the government holds strategic control to operating the subsectors.[10] The aviation subsector is managed by the Civil Aviation Agency (CAA) directly under the government. The CAA is responsible for the airports, and air traffic control, which were under the MOT before 2018.

---

[10]   ADB. Technical Assistance Consultant's Report: Country Governance Risk Assessment Tajikistan (TA9061 REG). Unpublished.

Figure 2: Transport Sector Organizational Structure

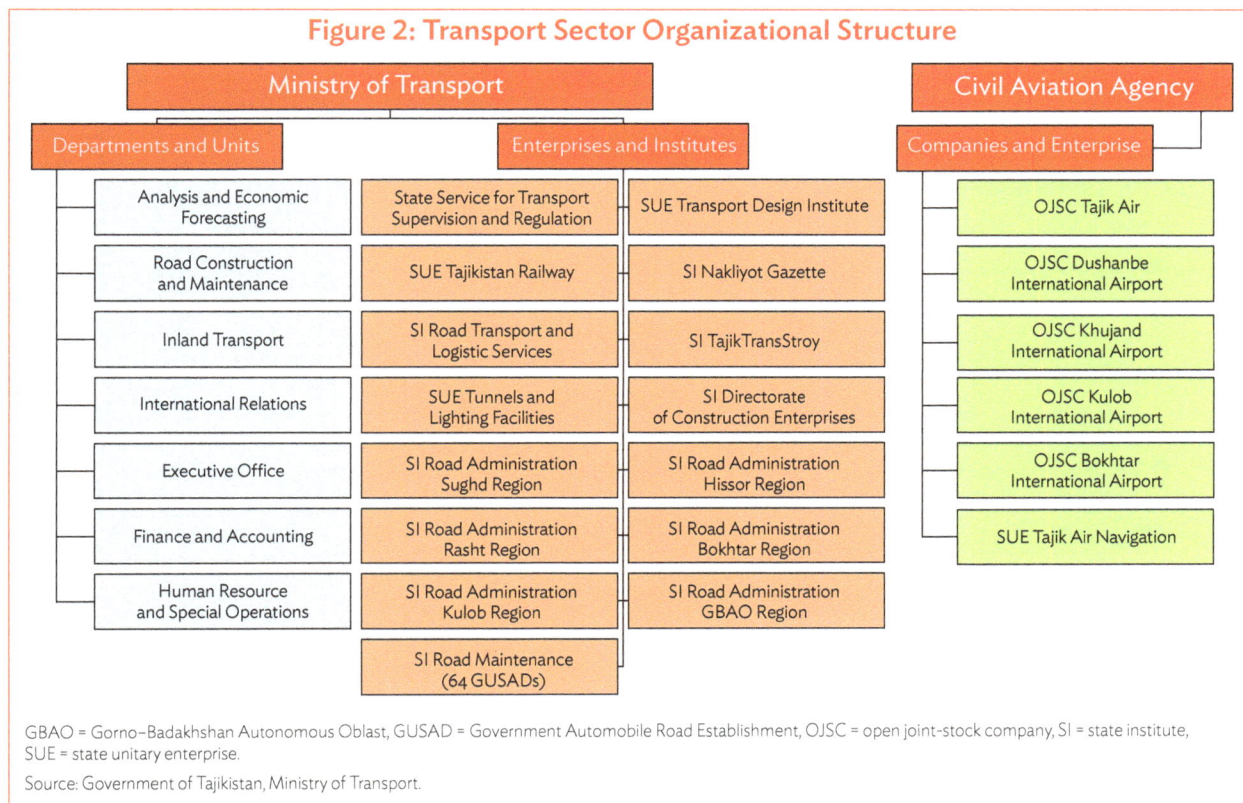

Ministry of Transport			Civil Aviation Agency	
Departments and Units	**Enterprises and Institutes**		**Companies and Enterprise**	
Analysis and Economic Forecasting	State Service for Transport Supervision and Regulation	SUE Transport Design Institute	OJSC Tajik Air	
Road Construction and Maintenance	SUE Tajikistan Railway	SI Nakliyot Gazette	OJSC Dushanbe International Airport	
Inland Transport	SI Road Transport and Logistic Services	SI TajikTransStroy	OJSC Khujand International Airport	
International Relations	SUE Tunnels and Lighting Facilities	SI Directorate of Construction Enterprises	OJSC Kulob International Airport	
Executive Office	SI Road Administration Sughd Region	SI Road Administration Hissor Region	OJSC Bokhtar International Airport	
Finance and Accounting	SI Road Administration Rasht Region	SI Road Administration Bokhtar Region	SUE Tajik Air Navigation	
Human Resource and Special Operations	SI Road Administration Kulob Region	SI Road Administration GBAO Region		
	SI Road Maintenance (64 GUSADs)			

GBAO = Gorno–Badakhshan Autonomous Oblast, GUSAD = Government Automobile Road Establishment, OJSC = open joint-stock company, SI = state institute, SUE = state unitary enterprise.

Source: Government of Tajikistan, Ministry of Transport.

14.   The State Service for Transport Supervision and Regulation, an agency under the MOT, is responsible for overseeing the transport sector, monitoring compliance with existing legislation, and regulating transport activities. The agency is responsible for business activities related to public transport services in roads and railways subsectors. It is also authorized to issue and renew licenses for contractors and transport service operators to carry out their services and works in the country, including construction, rehabilitation, and reconstruction of transport infrastructure; carriage of passengers and cargos; and design and research works relevant to the transport sector. Utilizing specific vehicles requires licenses issued by the agency. The SUE Design Institute for Transport Infrastructure is responsible for technical designs, testing, and research in the transport sector. The State Institute Nakliyot Gazette publishes the transportation newsletter.[11]

Road Subsector

15.   The MOT's Economic Analysis and Forecasting Department and Road Construction and Maintenance Department are actively involved in managing the roads under the MOT's jurisdiction. The Inland Transport Department includes the Road Transport Unit, which regulates road transport. On 31 December 2020, the Road and Transport Sectors Digitalization Unit was established. The unit is responsible for storing and managing the digitalized information of the country's transport infrastructure, not only limited to roads.

16.   Apart from the above departments and units, several state entities are involved in the road subsector. The State Institute Road Transport and Logistic Services manages transportation services in the road sector, including issuing waybills and consignments to operators of transportation and logistics services. The State

---

[11]   The state institute publishes the weekly newsletter "Nakliyot," which is posted on the MOT's website. Government of Tajikistan, Ministry of Transport. Weekly Newspaper "Nakliyot." https://www.mintrans.tj/tg/khaftanomai-nakliyot/.

Institute Directorate of Construction Enterprises carries out construction works on roads and associated assets that are not covered under large investment projects. The State Institute TajikTransStroy is also responsible for road construction and maintenance. The departments and state institutes under the MOT are responsible for policy making, programming, and implementation, which may cause a conflict of interest or overlaps in their responsibilities. The reform of the MOT has been discussed to address such underlying issues in the subsector.[12]

17.	There are also six state institutes representing the regional road administrations of the MOT in Sughd (Khujand), Hissor, Rasht, Bokhtar, Kulob, and Gorno–Badakhshan Autonomous Oblast (GBAO) (Khorug). Under these regional road administrations are 64 State Institutes for Road Maintenance (Government Automobile Road Establishments [GUSADs]) at the district level. The SUE Supervision of Tunnels and Lighting Facilities, responsible for managing tunnels and lighting facilities in international and republican roads, was recently established.

18.	In addition to the MOT and the underlying state institutes and SUEs, other entities are also involved in the road subsector operation. The local authorities participate in managing local roads. The Ministry of Internal Affairs includes the traffic police, which is responsible for road traffic management and issuance of driving licenses (paras. 60 and 61). The customs service under the government administers border crossing points (BCPs) located along the road and railway infrastructure.

Rail Subsector

19.	The Inland Transport Department under the MOT also includes the Rail Transport Unit, which regulates railway transport. The management of the railways and rolling stocks is carried out by the SUE Tajikistan Railways.

Aviation Subsector

20.	The CAA is responsible for the management and oversight of the subsector. The SUE Tajik Air Navigation is in charge of air traffic control. Former SUEs in the aviation subsector have been transformed into OJSCs such as Tajik Air, the national airline established during the Soviet period, and the four international airports in Dushanbe,[13] Khujand, Kulob, and Bokhtar. The responsibility for operating those airports were originally established under the MOT and the SUE Tajik Air Navigation but were transferred to the CAA in 2018. Currently, the MOT does not have a department or unit specifically for overseeing the aviation subsector.

2.3 Development Partner Support

21.	Tajikistan's transport sector has received various financial and technical assistance from multilateral and bilateral donors and their relevant agencies. Multilateral development partners include ADB, the Asian Infrastructure Investment Bank, the European Bank for Reconstruction and Development (EBRD), the Islamic Development Bank, the OPEC Fund for International Development, and the World Bank. Bilateral donors have also been active in the transport sector, especially the PRC, which has financed several large projects. Meanwhile, various countries have extended assistance, including France, Iran, Japan, Kuwait, the PRC, Saudi Arabia, United Arab Emirates, and the United States. A summary of the investments by development partners and by sectors is presented in Table 1. The total investment of development partners in 2000–2020 amounts to nearly $2.6 billion, most of which are for the road subsector. A full list of the main development partner projects in the transport sector is provided in Appendix 1.

---

[12]	In 2017, the EBRD carried out a study, *Review of Road Standards and Road Sector Institutional Reform*, under its financed Dushanbe–Uzbekistan Border Road Improvement Project.

[13]	The OJSC Dushanbe International Airport oversees the operation of the Khorug Airport.

Table 1: Development Partner Financing in the Transport Sector, 2000–2020
($ million)

Development Partner	Road		Air		Rail		Total
	Grant	Loan	Grant	Loan	Grant	Loan	
Multilateral Partners							
Aga Khan Foundation	7.8	–	–	–	–	–	**7.8**
Asian Development Bank	609.6	155.3	–	–	–	–	**764.9**
Asian Infrastructure Investment Bank	–	27.5	–	–	–	–	**27.5**
European Bank for Reconstruction and Development	2.5	219.0	–	10.9	–	–	**232.4**
Islamic Development Bank	–	85.2	–	–	–	–	**85.2**
OPEC Fund for International Development	–	106.5	–	–	–	–	**106.5**
World Bank	148.2	145.8	–	–	–	–	**294.0**
Bilateral Partners							
France	–	–	–	26.5	–	–	**26.5**
Japan	145.6	–	24.2	–	–	–	**169.8**
Saudi Arabia	–	56.0	–	–	–	–	**56.0**
People's Republic of China	32.9	551.0	–	–	–	72.0	**655.9**
Iran	21.0	21.2	–	–	–	–	**42.2**
Kuwait	–	58.8	–	–	–	–	**58.8**
United Arab Emirates	–	35.0	–	–	–	–	**35.0**
United States	28.0	–	–	–	–	–	**28.0**
Total	**995.6**	**1,456.3**	**24.2**	**37.4**	**-**	**72.0**	**2,585.5**
	2,451.9		**61.6**		**72.0**		

Source: Asian Development Bank and Government of Tajikistan, Ministry of Transport.

22.   Most of the investments have focused on the international road network, especially the Central Asia Regional Economic Cooperation (CAREC)[14] corridors and the Asian highways. The roads and the development partners are listed in Table 2.

Table 2: Major Road Subsector Investments by Development Partners

Road Code	Road Section	CAREC	AH	Development Partners
IR01	Dushanbe–Khujand–Uzbekistan Border	6	7	Iran, PRC
IR02	Dushanbe–Tursunzoda–Uzbekistan Border	3	65	ADB, AIIB, EBRD
IR04	Dushanbe–Vakhdat	2,3,5	65,66	PRC
IR04	Vakhdat–Dangara		66	PRC
IR04	Kulob–Kalaikhumb		66	ADFD, IDB, Kuwait, OFID, Saudi Arabia
IR04	Murgob–Kulma–PRC Border		66	IDB
IR07	Vakhdat–Karamyk–Kyrgyz Republic Border	2,3,5	65	ADB, EBRD, OFID
IR09	Dushanbe–Kyzylkala–Bokhtar	2,5	7	ADB, OFID
IR09	Bokhtar–Dusti–Panji Poyon–Afghanistan Border	2,5	7	Japan, US
IR10	Bokhtar–Dangara			ADB, OFID
IR12	Dehmoy–Proletarsk–Uzbekistan Border			World Bank
IR13	Ayni–Panjakent–Uzbekistan Border	6		ADB, OFID
IR14	Dehmoy–Gafurov, Gafurov– Kistevarz, Kuchkak–Konibodom, Konibodom–Patar			World Bank

(continued on next page)

---

14   The CAREC member countries are Afghanistan, Azerbaijan, Georgia, Kazakhstan, the Kyrgyz Republic, Mongolia, Pakistan, the People's Republic of China, Tajikistan, Turkmenistan, and Uzbekistan.

(Table 2 continued)

Road Code	Road Section	CAREC	AH	Development Partners
IR16	Isfara–Guliston–Uzbekistan Border			World Bank
RR026	Dangara–Kangurt			PRC
RR030	Hulbuk–Temurmalik			ADB
RR031	Temurmalik –Kangurt			ADB
RR032	Vose–Khovaling			ADB
RR054	Dangara–Okmazor			ADB
RR069	Kim–Isfara			World Bank
RR091	Kurkat–Bekobod			World Bank
RR	Kuchkak–Kim			World Bank

ADB = Asian Development Bank, ADFD = Abu Dhabi Fund for Development, AH = Asian highway, AIIB = Asian Infrastructure Investment Bank, CAREC = Central Asia Regional Economic Cooperation, EBRD = European Bank for Reconstruction and Development, IDB = Islamic Development Bank, IR = international road, OFID = OPEC Fund for International Development, PRC = People's Republic of China, RR = republican road, US = United States.

Notes:

1. Bokhtar was formerly known as Kurgonteppa.

2. The list includes the sections where civil works have not yet commenced and interventions of rehabilitating and constructing tunnels and bridges.

Source: Technical assistance consultants.

3. Sector and Subsector Assessment

23.   This chapter examines the transport sector before discussing in detail the four subsectors of roads, railways, aviation, and cross-border and logistics facilitation.

3.1 Transport Sector Context

24.   Tajikistan is a landlocked and mountainous country in Central Asia with geographical challenges and disaster-prone nature, complicating transport. The dominant transport infrastructure is road, which plays a key role in facilitating domestic and international connectivity. Road connectivity is oriented mainly toward Uzbekistan, accounting for more than half of the main road border crossing points (BCPs), as well as the Kyrgyz Republic through several BCPs. The railway network dates from the Soviet period and is also oriented toward Uzbekistan (all four railway border crossings are with Uzbekistan). The central and southern railway networks were connected in 2016, but the northern network remains accessible only through Uzbekistan. Four international airports are in Dushanbe, Khujand, Kulob, and Bokhtar. Although there are several domestic airports, only the airports in Dushanbe, Khujand, and Khorug operate scheduled domestic flights. The transport network in the country is presented in Map 1.

25.   The nearest seaport—Bandar Abbas, Iran—can be accessed through Afghanistan, but the available transport modes to reach the port are limited.[15] Access can also be achieved through Uzbekistan and Turkmenistan, which have road and rail access. However, traders and transporters from Tajikistan have experienced difficulties in their access to the seaport due to some blockages and economic sanctions imposed to Iran. Alternative options are (i) through Uzbekistan and Kazakhstan to the Caspian Sea; and (ii) either across to Baku in Azerbaijan and down to the Persian Gulf through Iran, or across to Georgia and west to the Black Sea. These routes are quite circuitous, increasing transport costs and times. Although transport by road to the east toward the PRC is possible, it is complicated due to the mountainous terrain, making it costly and time-consuming. A rail connection to the PRC is possible through Uzbekistan and Kazakhstan, but it is also inefficient and costly.

26.   Tajikistan has good connectivity to Kazakhstan and the Russian Federation with road and rail connections through Uzbekistan and/or the Kyrgyz Republic. These countries are considered key trading partners and important destinations for passengers. Air transport has connectivity to the neighboring and regional countries, and the major destination is the Russian Federation, with 0.52 million Tajik migrants in 2019.[16]

---

[15]   The construction of a new railway through Afghanistan was agreed in 2013, and the construction of a new railway bridge at Panji Poyon was confirmed in 2020.

[16]   ADB. 2020. *Strengthening Support for Labor Migration in Tajikistan: Assessment and Recommendations.* Manila.

Map 1: Transport Network in Tajikistan

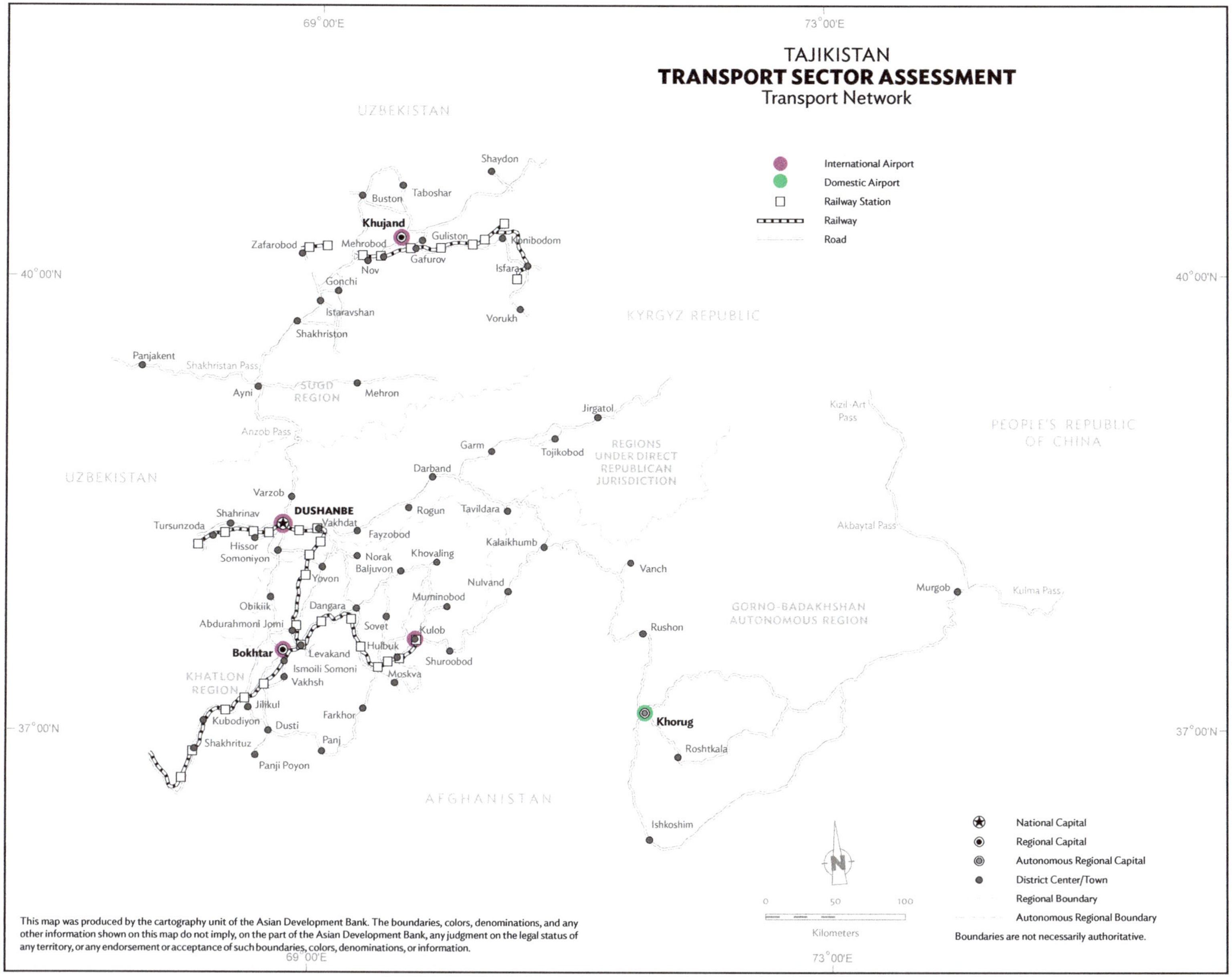
TAJIKISTAN
TRANSPORT SECTOR ASSESSMENT
Transport Network
International Airport
Domestic Airport
Railway Station
Railway
Road
National Capital
Regional Capital
Autonomous Regional Capital
District Center/Town
Regional Boundary
Autonomous Regional Boundary
Boundaries are not necessarily authoritative.
0 50 100
Kilometers
69°00'E
73°00'E
40°00'N
37°00'N
UZBEKISTAN
KYRGYZ REPUBLIC
PEOPLE'S REPUBLIC OF CHINA
AFGHANISTAN
SUGD REGION
KHATLON REGION
REGIONS UNDER DIRECT REPUBLICAN JURISDICTION
GORNO-BADAKHSHAN AUTONOMOUS REGION
DUSHANBE
Khujand
Bokhtar
Khorug
Shaydon
Taboshar
Buston
Zafarobod
Mehrobod
Guliston
Gafurov
Nov
Konibodom
Isfara
Vorukh
Gonchi
Istaravshan
Shakhriston
Panjakent
Shakhristan Pass
Ayni
Mehron
Anzob Pass
Varzob
Shahrinav
Tursunzoda
Hissor
Somoniyon
Vakhdat
Fayzobod
Rogun
Darband
Garm
Tojikobod
Jirgatol
Tavildara
Kalaikhumb
Norak
Baljuvon
Khovaling
Yovon
Nulvand
Muminobod
Obikiik
Dangara
Abdurahmoni Jomi
Sovet
Kulob
Hulbuk
Levakand
Ismoili Somoni
Vakhsh
Shuroobod
Moskva
Jilikul
Kubodiyon
Dusti
Farkhor
Panj
Shakhrituz
Panji Poyon
Vanch
Rushon
Roshtkala
Ishkoshim
Murgob
Kizil-Art Pass
Akbaytal Pass
Kulma Pass
This map was produced by the cartography unit of the Asian Development Bank. The boundaries, colors, denominations, and any other information shown on this map do not imply, on the part of the Asian Development Bank, any judgment on the legal status of any territory, or any endorsement or acceptance of such boundaries, colors, denominations, or information.

Source: Asian Development Bank.

Passenger Transport

27.   The volume of passenger transport has been increasing on average by 8% per year, quadrupling from 150 million in 2000 to more than 600 million in 2018. Road transport is the primary travel mode for passengers, accounting for more than 99% of the total passenger volume. Air and railway transport are responsible for only a tiny portion of total passenger transport. Table 3 shows the recent trends of the passenger volumes in 2000–2018 (total of international and domestic volumes), revealing the most significant increase in road transport.

Table 3: Passenger Volumes, 2000–2018
(million passengers)

Mode	2000	2001	2002	2003	2004	2005	2006	2007	2008	2009	2010	2011	2012	2013	2014	2015	2016	2017	2018
Road	150	171	225	264	339	397	414	428	454	514	538	541	519	543	555	563	572	593	613
Rail	1.0	0.4	0.5	0.5	0.7	0.7	0.7	0.8	0.8	0.7	0.6	0.6	0.5	0.5	0.5	0.4	0.5	0.5	0.5
Air	0.2	0.3	0.4	0.4	0.6	0.5	0.4	0.6	0.7	0.7	0.8	0.8	1.0	1.1	1.1	0.8	0.8	0.9	0.8
Total	151	172	226	265	340	398	415	429	456	515	539	542	521	545	557	564	573	594	614

Note: Numbers may not sum precisely because of rounding.

Source: Statistics Agency under the President of the Republic of Tajikistan.

28.   The shares of international passenger transport are very different from the domestic one. International passenger transport is mainly by air (43%), followed by rail (29%) and road (28%). Table 4 shows the numbers of annual international passengers by travel. Migrant workers traveling to and from the Russian Federation or neighboring countries presumably make up most international passenger transport. This can be explained by the observation that the remittance from Tajik migrant workers outside the country forms more than 30% of the GDP in 2019 and that about 20% of the working-age population leaves the country for work (footnote 16).

Table 4: Annual International Passengers by Travel
(million passengers)

Mode	2014	2015	2016	2017	2018
Road	...	0.2	0.2	0.3	0.5
Rail	0.5	0.4	0.5	0.5	0.5
Air	1.1	0.8	0.8	0.9	0.8
Total	...	1.4	1.5	1.7	1.8

... = data not available.

Sources: Government of Tajikistan, Ministry of Transport; and ADB. 2021. *Railway Sector Assessment for Tajikistan*. Manila.

Freight Transport

29.   Freight transport has also been steadily increasing on average by 5% per year, from 21.2 million tons in 2014 to 25.5 million tons in 2018 (Table 5). Freight transport by road has risen sharply by 40.1% during 2014–2018, while freight transport by rail has dropped by 21.3%. The latter is partly attributed to the reduction in the freight volumes through the northern line. Although international freight transport continues to be mainly by rail transport, the share of road freight volumes has been gradually increasing from 16.8% in 2014 to 23.0% in 2018, suggesting that freight traders are shifting their transport mode to roads.

Table 5: Breakdown of Freight Transport by Road and Rail
(million tons)

Indicator	2014	2015	2016	2017	2018
Road Transport					
International	1.35	1.13	0.94	1.35	1.57
Domestic	13.02	14.15	15.08	16.71	18.57
Subtotal	**14.37**	**15.28**	**16.02**	**18.06**	**20.14**
Rail Transport					
International	6.70	5.94	5.35	4.53	5.25
Domestic	0.10	0.19	0.10	0.12	0.10
Subtotal	**6.80**	**6.13**	**5.45**	**4.65**	**5.35**
Total	**21.17**	**21.41**	**21.47**	**22.71**	**25.49**

Source: ADB. 2021. *Railway Sector Assessment for Tajikistan*. Manila.

30.   Tajikistan exports mainly mineral products and (precious) metals that together make up about 70% of the total export, amounting to $811 million in 2019 (Table 6). Products with large shares in value are gold (21.6% of the total export), raw aluminum (17.1%), and raw cotton (10.6%). The main export partners are Turkey, Switzerland, and Uzbekistan, accounting for more than 60% of all the exports in value, followed by Kazakhstan, the PRC, and the Russian Federation (Table 7). Exports to Uzbekistan have been increasing in value in recent years, and Uzbekistan is becoming one of the important export destinations.[17]

Table 6: Main Export and Import Products, 2019

Export ($811 million)		Import ($4,018 million)	
Products	**Share (%)**	**Products**	**Share (%)**
Gold	21.5	Refined petroleum	8.2
Raw aluminum	17.2	Wheat	5.1
Raw cotton	10.6	Petroleum gas	4.1
Zinc ore	9.0	Aluminum oxide	2.8
Other ores	6.3	Planes, helicopters, spacecraft	2.8
Non-retail pure cotton yarn	5.3	Raw iron bars	2.1
Others	30.1	Others	75.9
Total	**100.0**	**Total**	**100.0**

Source: Observatory of Economic Complexity. Tajikistan. https://oec.world/en/profile/country/tjk (accessed 20 October 2021).

Table 7: Main Export and Import Partners, 2019

Export ($811 million)		Import ($4,018 million)	
Destination Countries	**Share (%)**	**Origin Countries**	**Share (%)**
Turkey	23.5	People's Republic of China	40.1
Switzerland	21.6	Russian Federation	23.7
Uzbekistan	16.4	Kazakhstan	16.2
Kazakhstan	11.5	Uzbekistan	4.7

(continued on next page)

[17]   The export to Uzbekistan in value increased to $133 million in 2019 from $132 million in 2018, and the major products were zinc ore and cement, accounting for more than 50% of the total value. Observatory of Economic Complexity. Tajikistan. https://oec.world/en/profile/country/tjk (accessed 20 October 2021).

(Table 7 continued)

Export ($811 million)		Import ($4,018 million)	
Destination Countries	**Share (%)**	**Origin Countries**	**Share (%)**
People's Republic of China	10.2	Turkey	3.9
Russian Federation	4.4	United Arab Emirates	1.5
Others	12.4	Others	9.9
Total	**100.0**	**Total**	**100.0**

Source: Observatory of Economic Complexity. Tajikistan. https://oec.world/en/profile/country/tjk (accessed 20 October 2021).

31.　　In 2019, the total import of Tajikistan was valued at $4.02 billion. Products imported were quite varied, including refined petroleum, wheat, and metals. The PRC is the dominant import partner, accounting for 40.1% of the total value, followed by the Russian Federation (5.1%, mainly for refined petroleum) and Kazakhstan (2.8%, mainly for wheat and petroleum gas).

32.　　The total value of exports is about 20% of that of imports in 2019. This imbalance is also observed between the import origin and export destination countries: exports are mainly to the north and west of Tajikistan, such as Turkey, Switzerland, Uzbekistan, while imports are from the east and north of the country, including the PRC, the Russian Federation, and Kazakhstan. Such asymmetrical trade flows make it difficult to organize round trips, raising transportation costs. Imports and exports are mainly by railway in northward-oriented transport since the railway lines are well connected in those directions. For trade with Europe and Turkey, existing blockages on the route may complicate railway transport, and thus road transport becomes more essential than ever. International freight transport includes a rather limited set of export products destined for a limited number of countries. As for imports from the PRC, trucks are mainly used due to the absence of direct rail network between the two countries, or goods are shipped to nearby seaports and subsequently transported by railway and/or road.

33.　　Kazakhstan and the Russian Federation are important trading partners, especially for importing petroleum products and wheat and the export of mineral products and metals. Railway transport is relatively straightforward through Uzbekistan directly to Kazakhstan and onward to Moscow and other regions of the Russian Federation. The railway route is highly competitive, especially for bulk products. Only for relatively short routes to southern Kazakhstan and involving high-value non-bulk shipments does road transport become competitive.

34.　　From the PRC, consumer goods such as rubber footwear, textiles, and clothing are imported. However, the trade route is complicated. Although Tajikistan has a border with the PRC (Kulma Pass), the access is through mountainous terrain and then only to the west end of the PRC, requiring further travel to economic centers of the PRC. A preferable transport option would therefore involve shipping to a nearby seaport. The nearest seaport for Tajikistan is Bandar Abbas in Iran, which can be accessed by train through Uzbekistan, Turkmenistan, and Iran. However, the route would involve complications for Tajik traders and transporters, including a gauge change in Iran that has standard gauge tracks. The alternative seaport is the Black Sea port of Batumi in Georgia. To access Batumi, the traders and transporters go to Aktau in Kazakhstan by rail through Uzbekistan, to Baku in Azerbaijan by rail ferry across the Caspian Sea, and then cross Azerbaijan and Georgia by railway. ADB (2021)[18] estimates that this circuitous route doubles the cost of freight transport from $5,000 per 60-ton wagon to nearly $10,000. This is partly because of the high tariffs charged on the railway network of countries belonging to the Eurasian Economic Union.[19] These high tariffs possibly affect the competitiveness of railway transport against road transport. Using the circuitous route through Kazakhstan, ADB (footnote 18) estimates that the cost per ton ($9,780 when using a 60-ton wagon, or $163/ton) is almost the same as the one for road transport ($170/ton).

---

[18]　ADB. 2021. *Railway Sector Assessment for Tajikistan*. Manila.

[19]　The member countries of the Eurasian Economic Union are Armenia, Belarus, Kazakhstan, the Kyrgyz Republic, and the Russian Federation.

35.   Other important trading partners are Turkey, which imports mainly raw aluminum, and European countries. The route through Uzbekistan and Kazakhstan by rail may be taken, crossing the Caspian Sea by ferry and continuing through Azerbaijan and Georgia to reach Turkey. This route requires a gauge change in Turkey. For the route to Turkey, rail transport may be advantageous against road transport since the total distance of the route by road is not quite shorter.

3.2 Road Subsector

36.   Due to the mountainous terrain and the fragmented railway network, roads are the dominant transport mode for domestic transport in Tajikistan. The road subsector's flexibility to demand and available route options make it increasingly important even for international transport.

Road Network

37.   The Law on Roads and Road Activities (Law No. 47, 2007) distinguishes public roads of national importance linking to neighboring countries (international roads) and connecting cities and towns (republican roads) from local roads including streets and rural roads. These roads are all registered in the MOT's State Register of Roads.

38.   Tajikistan has a road network of approximately 26,600 km, of which 14,339 km are public roads under the MOT's jurisdiction,[20] including 3,348 km of international roads (23.3%), 2,127 km of republican roads (14.8%), and 8,864 km of local roads (61.9%) (Table 8). About 70% of the road network is paved (89% of international roads, 77% of republican roads, and 65% of local roads). One-third of the country's road network (by length) has an asphalt concrete surface. The length share of asphalt concrete surface roads is 55.3% for international roads, 50.1% for republican roads, and 21.9% for local roads. Around 60% of the network is surfaced with bituminous gravel or gravel; the remaining are unpaved roads, predominantly local roads. The pavement surface type per the road category is shown in Figure 3.

Table 8: Road Network by Category and Surface Type
(km)

Category	Asphalt	Bituminous Gravel	Gravel	Unpaved	Total
International	1,851	1,142	353	2	3,348
Republican	1,065	564	462	36	2,127
Local	1,941	3,789	1,995	1,139	8,864
Total	**4,857**	**5,495**	**2,810**	**1,177**	**14,339**

km = kilometer.

Source: Government of Tajikistan, Ministry of Transport.

---

[20]   The remaining 12,261 km of roads are private industrial roads and access roads that are managed by different ministries, agencies, local governments, and private companies.

Figure 3: Road Network in Tajikistan by Category and Surface Type (km)

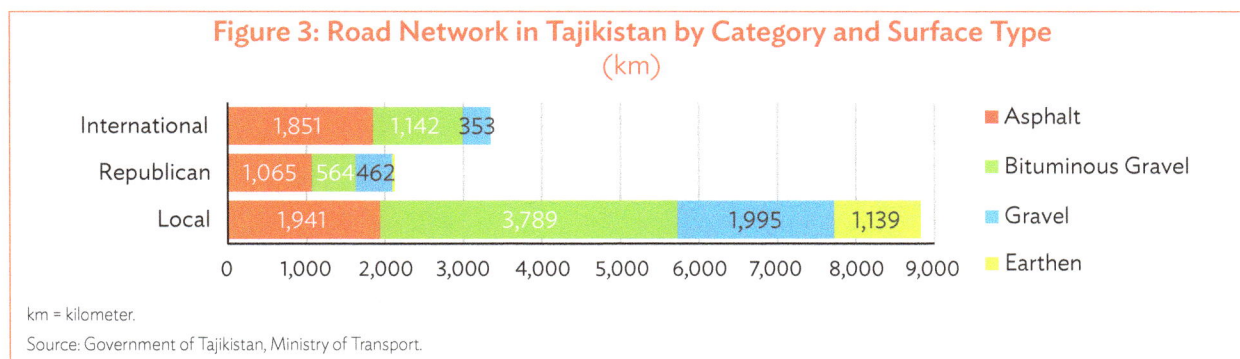

km = kilometer.

Source: Government of Tajikistan, Ministry of Transport.

39.   The State Register of Roads identifies 19 international roads and 98 republican roads.[21] Most of the international roads are along the CAREC corridors (Map 2) and the Asian highways (Map 2). The international roads are listed in Table 9 and the republican roads in Appendix 2.

Table 9: List of International Roads

Code	International Roads	Length (km)	CAREC Corridor	Asian Highway
IR 01	Dushanbe–Chanok (via Khujand–Buston–Uzbekistan border)	368.20	6	7
IR 02	Dushanbe–Tursunzoda–Uzbekistan Border	66.30	3	65
IR 03	Labijar–Tavildara–Darvoz	135.00		
IR 04	Dushanbe–Kulma Pass (via Vakhdat–Kulob–Khorug–Murgob–PRC Border)	1,008.66		66
IR 05	Murgob–Kyzylart Pass–Kyrgyz Republic Border	187.00		
IR 06	Khorug– Ishkoshim –Tuzkul (access to Dushanbe–Kulma Highway)	320.40		
IR 07	Vakhdat–Rasht–Jirgatol–Kyrgyz Republic Border	319.00	2, 3, 5	65
IR 08	Gulistan–Farkhor–Panj–Dusti	140.80		
IR 09	Dushanbe–Bokhtar–Panji Poyon–Afghanistan Border (Bridge)	181.30	2, 5	7
IR 10	Bokhtar–Sarband–Dangara	76.10		
IR 11	Kyzylkala–Kubodiyon –Shakhrituz–Aiwanj–Afghanistan Border	168.20		
IR 12	Proletar village–Isfana–Kyrgyz Republic Border	9.40		
IR 13	Ayni–Panjakent–Uzbekistan Border	112.70	6	
IR 14	Konibodom–Dehmoy (access to Dushanbe-Chanok Highway)	98.40		
IR 15	Istaravshan–Zafarobod –Uzbekistan Border	28.00		
IR 16	Isfara–Batken (to the Kyrgyz Republic Border)	10.00		
IR 17	Isfara–Vorukh (to the Kyrgyz Republic Border)	43.90		
IR 18	Isfara–Dahana (to the Uzbekistan Border)	24.50		
IR 19	Ghafurov–Qahramon–Pungan–Uzbekistan Border	122.00		

CAREC = Central Asia Regional Economic Cooperation, IR = international road, km = kilometer, PRC = People's Republic of China.

Source: Compiled by the technical assistance consultant based on the information provided by Tajikistan's Ministry of Transport.

40.   The road network also includes 5 major tunnels[22] with a combined length of 18 km and a further 10 km of galleries, 2,252 bridges with a combined length of 43.7 km, as well as 19,714 culverts with a combined length of 213.0 km (Table 10).

---

[21]   The road lengths in the State Register of Roads are slightly different from actual lengths, as the register is updated only once every 5 years and was last updated in 2015.

[22]   The five tunnels are (i) Dusti, 1.047 km; (ii) Anzob (Istiklol), 5.040 km; (iii) Shahristan, 5.253 km along IR01; (iv) Khatlon (Chormagzak), 4.450 km; and (v) Ozodi (Shar-Shar), 2.250 km along IR04.

Map 2: Central Asia Regional Economic Cooperation Corridors

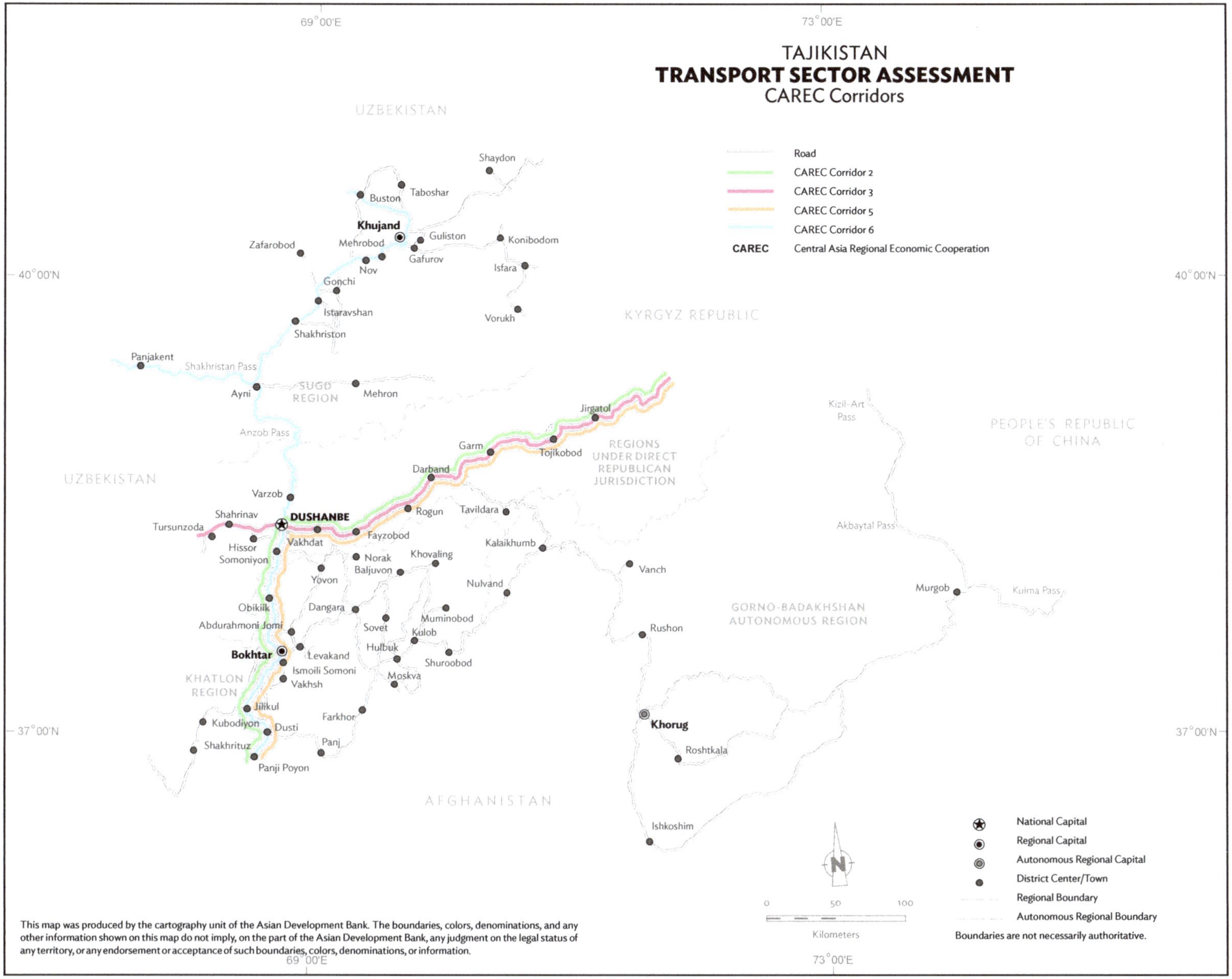

TAJIKISTAN
TRANSPORT SECTOR ASSESSMENT
CAREC Corridors

Road
CAREC Corridor 2
CAREC Corridor 3
CAREC Corridor 5
CAREC Corridor 6

CAREC   Central Asia Regional Economic Cooperation

National Capital
Regional Capital
Autonomous Regional Capital
District Center/Town
Regional Boundary
Autonomous Regional Boundary

Boundaries are not necessarily authoritative.

UZBEKISTAN

KYRGYZ REPUBLIC

PEOPLE'S REPUBLIC OF CHINA

AFGHANISTAN

SUGD REGION

KHATLON REGION

REGIONS UNDER DIRECT REPUBLICAN JURISDICTION

GORNO-BADAKHSHAN AUTONOMOUS REGION

Panjakent
Zafarobod
Shakhriston
Istaravshan
Gonchi
Mehrobod
Buston
Nov
Khujand
Gafurov
Guliston
Taboshar
Shaydon
Konibodom
Istara
Vorukh
Mehron
Ayni
Varzob
Shakhriston Pass
Anzob Pass
Tursunzoda
Shahrinav
Hissor
Somoniyon
Obikiik
Abdurahmoni Jomi
DUSHANBE
Vakhdat
Yovon
Dangara
Norak
Baljuvon
Levakand
Ismoili Somoni
Bokhtar
Kubodiyon
Jilikul
Dusti
Shakhrituz
Panji Poyon
Panj
Farkhor
Vakhsh
Soviet
Hulbuk
Kulob
Moskva
Muminobod
Shurobod
Khovaling
Fayzobod
Rogun
Darband
Garm
Tavildara
Kalaikhumb
Nulvand
Vanch
Rushon
Jirgatol
Tojikobod
Khorug
Roshtkala
Ishkoshim
Murgob
Kuima Pass
Abbytal Pass
Kizil-Art Pass

0   50   100
Kilometers

N

Source: Asian Development Bank.

This map was produced by the cartography unit of the Asian Development Bank. The boundaries, colors, denominations, and any other information shown on this map do not imply, on the part of the Asian Development Bank, any judgment on the legal status of any territory, or any endorsement or acceptance of such boundaries, colors, denominations, or information.

69° 00'E   73° 00'E

40° 00'N   37° 00'N

Map 3: Asian Highways Networks

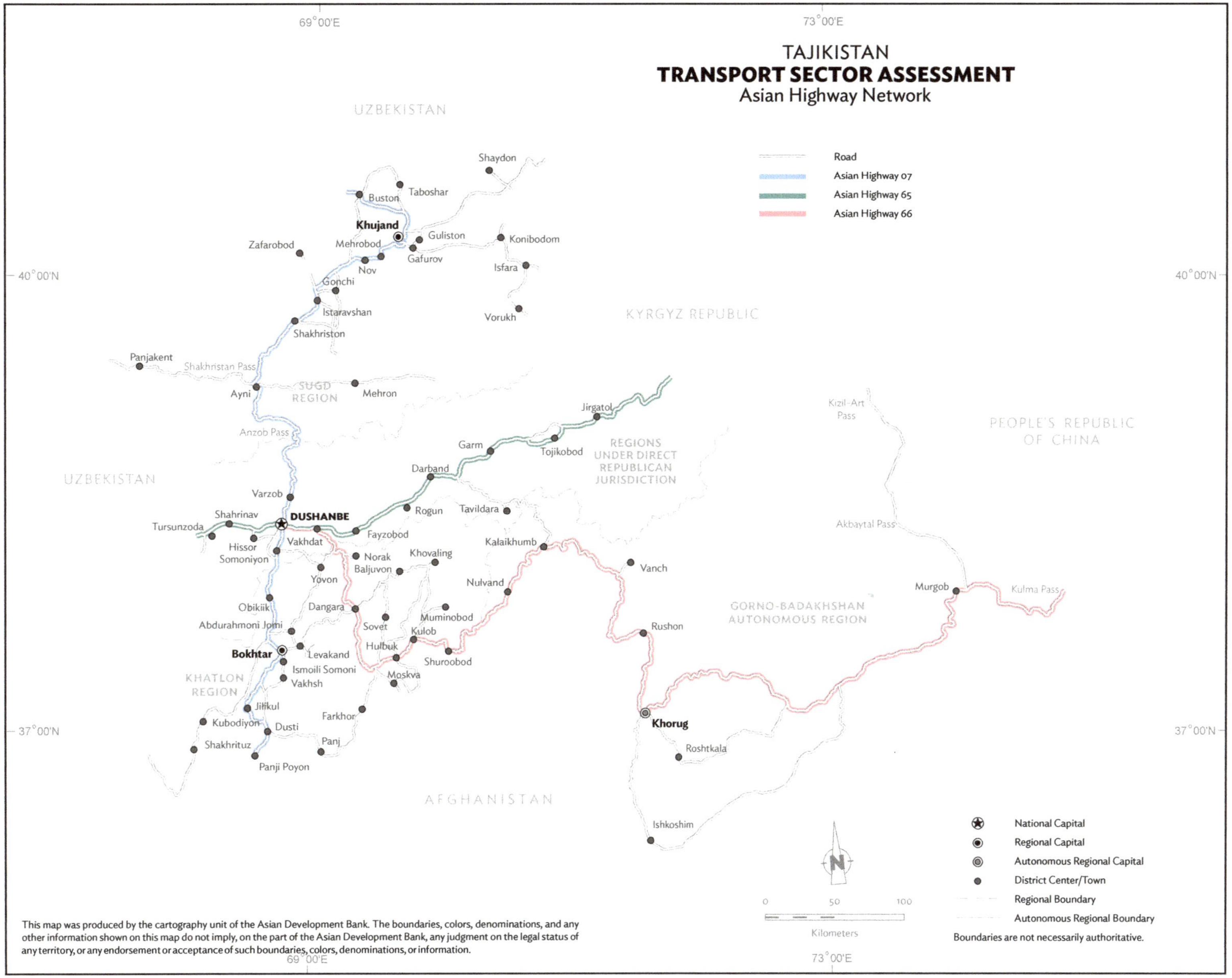

TAJIKISTAN
TRANSPORT SECTOR ASSESSMENT
Asian Highway Network

Road
Asian Highway 07
Asian Highway 65
Asian Highway 66

National Capital
Regional Capital
Autonomous Regional Capital
District Center/Town
Regional Boundary
Autonomous Regional Boundary
Boundaries are not necessarily authoritative.

UZBEKISTAN
KYRGYZ REPUBLIC
PEOPLE'S REPUBLIC OF CHINA
AFGHANISTAN

SUGD REGION
KHATLON REGION
REGIONS UNDER DIRECT REPUBLICAN JURISDICTION
GORNO-BADAKHSHAN AUTONOMOUS REGION

DUSHANBE
Khujand
Khorug
Bokhtar

Shaydon, Konibodom, Guliston, Isfara, Vorukh, Taboshar, Buston, Gafurov, Mehrobod, Nov, Gonchi, Istaravshan, Shakhriston, Zafarobod, Ayni, Mehron, Jirgatol, Garm, Tojikobod, Tavildara, Dartband, Rogun, Kalaikhumb, Nulvand, Vanch, Rushon, Murgob, Roshtkala, Ishkoshim, Kulob, Muminobod, Shuroobod, Khovaling, Baljuvon, Norak, Sovet, Hulbuk, Moskva, Farkhor, Panj, Fayzobod, Yovon, Dangara, Levakand, Ismoili Somoni, Vakhsh, Jilikul, Dusti, Panji Poyon, Kubodiyon, Shakhrituz, Abdurahmoni Jomi, Obikiik, Somoniyon, Hissor, Shahrinav, Varzob, Tursunzoda, Panjakent, Vakhdat

Shahriston Pass, Anzob Pass, Shakhristan Pass, Abbaytal Pass, Kizil-Art Pass, Kulmi Pass

Kilometers
0   50   100

73°00'E
69°00'E
40°00'N
37°00'N
37°00'N
40°00'N

This map was produced by the cartography unit of the Asian Development Bank. The boundaries, colors, denominations, and any other information shown on this map do not imply, on the part of the Asian Development Bank, any judgment on the legal status of any territory, or any endorsement or acceptance of such boundaries, colors, denominations, or information.

Source: Asian Development Bank

Table 10: Structures in Public Road Network

Category	Tunnels and Galleries		Bridges		Culverts	
	No.	Length (km)	No.	Length (km)	No.	Length (km)
International	5	28.3	515	15.4	5,282	74.0
Republican	–	–	333	8.1	2,900	32.7
Local	–	–	1,404	20.2	11,532	106.3
Total	**5**	**28.3**	**2,252**	**43.7**	**19,714**	**213.0**

km = kilometer.

Sources: Government of Tajikistan, Ministry of Transport; and Asian Development Bank.

41.   Most of the country's road network was constructed during the Soviet period. It was estimated in the NTDPTS that, in 2011, about 60%–80% of the network would require significant rehabilitation, with more than half the road length having an international roughness index greater than 7 meters (m) per km and an average travel speed of only 30 km per hour (km/h). The most recent road condition data from the MOT show a more positive picture, as shown in Table 11, with 56% of roads in poor condition. Poor road conditions are prevalent in local roads. One critical issue is improving the quality of roads at the design stage to avoid rapid deterioration.

Table 11: Estimated Road Conditions
(%)

Road Class	Good	Fair	Poor	Condition
International roads	18	39	43	18% / 39% / 43% ■ Good
Republican roads	10	31	59	10% / 31% / 59% ■ Fair
Local roads	9	25	66	9% / 25% / 66%
Total	**12**	**32**	**56**	12% / 32% / 56% ■ Poor

Source: Government of Tajikistan, Ministry of Transport.

42.   Development partners have been supporting the upgrade and rehabilitation of large portions of the CAREC corridors and Asian highways, improving the quality of international roads and, subsequently, international connectivity. Recently, development partners have extended their assistance in improving certain republican roads, which are essential for domestic connectivity. The improvement of republican roads focused on areas with high population density, especially in Sughd and Khatlon.[23]

43.   The country's road design standards are summarized in Table 12.

Table 12: Road Design Standards

	Category				
	I	II	III	IV	V
Average daily intensity of automobile traffic in both directions during a year	More than 7,000	3,000–7,000	1,000–3,000	200–1,000	Less than 2,000
Design speed, kilometer per hour	80–150	60–120	50–100	40–80	30–60
Number of lanes	4 and more	2	2	2	1
Width a lane (m)	3.75	3.75	3.5	3	–
Width of roadways (m)	15 and more	7.5	7	6	4.5
Width of a roadside (m)	3.75	3.75	2.5	2	1.75

(continued on next page)

[23]   Statistics Agency under the President of the Republic of Tajikistan. 2020. *Population of the Republic of Tajikistan as of 1 January 2020*. Dushanbe. In 2020, the country's total population is 9.31 million–3.35 million (36.0% of the total population) in Khatlon Oblast and 2.71 million (29.1%) in the Sughd Oblast. The oblasts' population density (135.6 per square kilometers [km²] for the Khatlon Oblast and 107.4/km² for the Sughd Oblast) is higher than the country's average of 65.9/km².

(Table 12 continued)

	Category				
	I	**II**	**III**	**IV**	**V**
Road top with (grading width) (m)	27.5	15	12	10	8
Maximum longitudinal slope (%)	30–60	40–70	50–80	60–90	70–100

m = meter.

Source: Russian Construction Codes and Regulations 02.0585.

Road Construction and Maintenance

44.   The roads under the MOT's jurisdiction, international and republican roads, are managed by the MOT's concerned departments and units, while the implementation of routine and winter maintenance is primarily carried out through 6 regional road administrations[24] and 64 state institutes for road maintenance (GUSADs) at the district level. Larger works such as construction and rehabilitation are carried out by the State Institute Directorate of Construction Enterprises for the government-financed works or contracted out to private contractors for the works that receive finances from development partners. Meanwhile, the district, city and town authorities are in charge of local roads and chronically face insufficient financial resources and technical expertise for regular maintenance. Therefore, the MOT helps in maintaining some local roads, particularly those which are considered essential.

45.   The GUSADs are responsible for routine and winter maintenance of the roads in their districts, with road lengths ranging from 70 km to 640 km. The number of staff is correspondingly varied between 24 and 97. The GUSADs are classified as category IV contractors[25] and are thus not allowed to carry out larger works. In 2020, the MOT reported that the total number of staff of the 64 GUSADs is 2,741 and it owns 1,619 pieces of machinery and equipment, including 516 pieces of machinery. (Table 13). Some of the GUSADs have received new equipment with support from development partners.

Table 13: Road Length, Number of Government Automobile Road Establishments, and Staff by Regional Road Administration Office

Regional Office	Hissor	Kulob	Bokhtar	Sughd	GBAO	Rasht	Total
International/Republican roads (km)	680	748	770	1,149	1,660	469	5,476
Local roads (km)	1,235	1,696	1,981	2,415	1,068	468	8,863
Total (km)	**1,915**	**2,444**	**2,751**	**3,564**	**2,728**	**937**	**14,339**
GUSADs (no.)	9	11	13	14	10	7	64
Staff (regional)	26	27	25	27	26	23	154
Staff (GUSADs)	322	467	497	675	558	222	2,741

GBAO = Gorno–Badakhshan Autonomous Oblast, GUSAD = Government Automobile Road Establishment, km = kilometer.

Note: Murgob district in GBAO covers a third of the total territory of Tajikistan and has 640 km of roads.

Source: Government of Tajikistan, Ministry of Transport.

46.   Larger road works financed by the government are carried out by the State Institute Directorate of Construction Enterprises. Those financed by development partners are carried out by contractors as governed by their procurement regulations. Apart from the GUSADs, there are approximately 190 private contractors registered in Tajikistan (including 18 international companies) and 80 state-owned companies.[26] The private contractors are generally category III and higher, while the state-owned contractors are relatively small and are considered to be as category IV contractors.

---

[24]   The regional road administrators are established as state institutes under the MOT in Sughd, Hissor, Rasht, Bokhtar, Kulob, and GBAO. The total number of staff in the 6 regional road administrators is 154, as detailed in Appendix 3.

[25]   Category IV contractors are defined in the EBRD's GUSAD's Transformation Report (unpublished) as such: "Organizations are entitled to conduct off-carriageway works, works on roads of about 1 km, works on farm roads, kolhozes, and check the condition of construction. They can carry out visual checks of constructions and provide information on defects and recommendations on further capital repairs."

[26]   EBRD. GUSAD's Transformation Report. Unpublished.

47.   There are two sets of pilot experiences with output- and performance-based maintenance. The first pilot experience involved two output- and performance-based road contracts where contractors were responsible for both initial works and subsequent winter and routine maintenance. According to the contract documents, these two output- and performance-based road contract pilots were for 3 years and carried out in the Vakhdat–Obigarm section (73 km) and the Nurobod–Nimich section (76 km), with costs averaging TJS41,934/km/year (TJS31,892/km/year excluding initial repairs). The second pilot involved 3-year performance-based maintenance contracts without initial repair works for the two sections of Sayron–Karamyk (89 km) and Vose–Khovaling (87 km), with costs averaging TJS13,088/km/year.[27] Routine maintenance was paid on a performance basis, while winter and emergency maintenance were paid on a volume basis against a work order issued by the MOT.

48.   The road from Dushanbe to Khujand continuing to the border with Uzbekistan at Chanak is under a 30-year concession. This road is 337 km long (the large tunnels are not included in the concession contract, nor are the sections within Dushanbe and Khujand).[28] The upgrading of this road, including the Dusti and Shahristan tunnels, was financed with a $281 million loan from the PRC, while the Anzob tunnel was financed with a $37 million loan and grant from Iran. The road maintenance, including all routine, winter, and periodic maintenance, is carried out by a local private company under a concession contract and financed from the toll revenue.

Road Subsector Funding

49.   The government budget allocations to the MOT for the road subsector vary yearly. Local governments also receive funding for the road subsector. The government funding is complemented by financial assistance from development partners, accounting for more than half of the road subsector funding during 2015–2019. Road user charges are collected but are channeled into the country's general budget instead of being ring-fenced for roads. The maintenance budget is also financed from different sources, including revenues that MOT enterprises (GUSADs and others) receive for services provided to other entities and the private sector. Total road subsector funding has been increasing, almost doubling in Tajik somoni terms during 2015–2019 (Table 14).

Table 14: Road Subsector Funding by Source of Funding
(TJS million)

Source of funding	2015	2016	2017	2018	2019
Ministry of Transport budget	188.0	125.4	235.1	159.1	455.9
Development partners	711.6	727.9	754.4	1,022.1	941.6
Local government	73.9	69.9	76.6	89.8	317.6
Other	13.5	25.1	8.8	29.2	36.4
Total	**987.0**	**948.3**	**1,074.9**	**1,300.2**	**1,751.5**
Total ($)	160.2	121.0	125.7	142.1	183.8

Note: The annual average exchange rate in the Asian Development Bank's Key Indicator for Asia and Pacific 2020 (https://data.adb.org/media/6521/download) was used for converting the amount in Tajik somoni into US dollars.

Source: Government of Tajikistan, Ministry of Transport.

50.   Increases in the road maintenance funding have not materialized at the same pace (Table 15). Funding is dependent on the general budget and outlays by local governments. Road maintenance funding made up 26% of total road government subsector funding in 2015, but by 2019 this had reduced to 10%.

---

[27]   These two road sections were recently rehabilitated under the CAREC Corridors 3 and 5 Enhancement Project. The unit rate shown for both pilot cases was calculated based on the contract and this report: ADB. 2015. *SC 104781 REG: Stocktaking of Road Maintenance in Central and West Asia–Stocktaking of Pilot Performance Based Road Maintenance Contracts in Tajikistan: Final Report.*

[28]   The MOT is responsible for operating and maintaining the tunnels.

Table 15: Road Maintenance Funding by Source of Funding
(TJS million)

Source of funding	2015	2016	2017	2018	2019
Ministry of Transport budget	59.6	57.8	60.2	60.8	68.6
Local government	9.6	11.1	8.7	8.9	10.0
Total	**69.2**	**68.9**	**68.9**	**69.7**	**78.6**
Total ($)	11.2	8.8	8.1	7.6	8.2

Note: The annual average exchange rate in the Asian Development Bank's Key Indicator for Asia and Pacific 2020 (https://data.adb.org/media/6521/download) was used for converting the amount in Tajik somoni into US dollars.

Source: Government of Tajikistan, Ministry of Transport.

51.   The reduction in road maintenance funding relative to the MOT's overall budget has been more pronounced, from 32% in 2015 to 15% in 2019.[29] Although funding levels in Tajik somoni have doubled during 2015–2019, they have remained more or less constant in US dollar (Table 16). Budget allocations for road maintenance are not increasing in line with inflation, as evidenced in the reduction in US dollar terms. In addition, the continuous growth in traffic volume and expansion of the country's road network requires more road maintenance budgets than before, which is not adequately reflected. This issue poses a serious risk to the road network sustainability and the improvements carried out in the past decades.

Table 16: Ministry of Transport Road Maintenance Budgets
(million)

Item	2010	2011	2012	2013	2014	2015	2016	2017	2018	2019
Road maintenance budget (TJS)	34.0	39.0	46.8	50.6	57.2	59.6	57.8	60.2	60.8	68.6
Road maintenance budget ($)	7.8	8.5	9.9	10.6	11.6	9.7	7.4	7.0	6.6	7.2

Note: The annual average exchange rate in the Asian Development Bank's Key Indicator for Asia and Pacific 2020 (https://data.adb.org/media/6521/download) was used for converting the amount in Tajik somoni into US dollars.

Source: ADB. CAREC Corridors 2, 5, and 6 (Dushanbe–Kurgonteppa) Road Project. Consultant's report. TA 8945-TAJ. Unpublished.

52.   Of the available road maintenance funding, a large part goes to the payment of salaries and pension costs of the staff of the GUSADs (Table 17). This funding has been increasing every year (46.5% in 2019 compared with 38.4% in 2015), reflecting increases in salary levels.

Table 17: Road Maintenance Budget Allocation
(TJS million)

Budget Item	2015	2016	2017	2018	2019
Republican road maintenance	12.2	14.8	11.6	11.4	11.4
	(20.5%)	(23.5%)	(19.3%)	(18.7%)	(16.6%)
Local road maintenance	5.2	6.3	5.0	4.9	4.9
	(8.7%)	(10.0%)	(8.3%)	(8.0%)	(7.1%)
Major repairs	3.6	3.6	3.2	3.2	3.2
	(6.0%)	(5.7%)	(5.3%)	(5.3%)	(4.7%)
Salaries	18.3	20.7	22.0	22.2	25.5
	(30.7%)	(32.8%)	(36.5%)	(36.5%)	(37.2%)
Social Protection Fund[a]	4.6	5.2	5.5	5.6	6.4
	(7.7%)	(8.3%)	(9.2%)	(9.2%)	(9.3%)
Centralized funds	12.6	9.4	10.0	10.5	14.0

(continued on next page)

---

[29]   In 2015, TJS59.6 million was allocated for maintaining the roads under the MOT's jurisdiction, accounting for 31.7% of the MOT's total budget of TJS188.0 million. In 2019, TJS68.6 million was allocated for maintaining those roads, representing 15.0% of the MOT's total budget of TJS455.9 million.

(Table 17 continued)

Budget Item	2015	2016	2017	2018	2019
	(21.2%)	(14.9%)	(16.6%)	(17.2%)	(20.4%)
Other costs	3.1	3.0	2.9	3.1	3.2
	(5.2%)	(4.8%)	(4.8%)	(5.1%)	(4.7%)
Total	**59.6**	**63.0**	**60.2**	**60.9**	**68.6**

ᵃ   Social Protection Fund includes pensions, social insurance, and employees' contributions.

Notes:

1.   Numbers may not sum precisely because of rounding.

2.   Percentages may not total 100% because of rounding.

Source: Government of Tajikistan, Ministry of Transport.

53.   The road maintenance allocations form about 20% of the estimated needs and are equivalent to 0.1% of GDP. The neighboring countries spend about 0.4% of their GDP, as shown in Table 18. In the case of Tajikistan, this amount would be equivalent to an annual allocation of $35 million. Indeed, an analysis using the Highway Development and Management Model (HDM-4) carried out in 2017 revealed that a budget equivalent to 0.4% of GDP would be required to stabilize the condition of the road network, while the gradual improvement of the road network up to more than 50% of the network in good condition would require a budget equivalent to 0.7% of GDP (Figure 4).[30] The inadequate maintenance budget would adversely affect the country's road network in the long run.

Table 18: Road Maintenance Funding as Percentage of Gross Domestic Product, 2016

Country	GDP Nominal ($ billion)	Road Network (kilometer)	Budget ($ million)	Budget (% of GDP)
Tajikistan	7.9	14,146	7.7	0.09
Armenia	10.6	7,704	44.0	0.42
Georgia	14.0	6,824	60.0	0.43
Kyrgyz Republic	6.6	18,585	29.3	0.45

GDP = gross domestic product.

Source: ADB. CAREC Corridors 2, 5, and 6 (Dushanbe–Kurgonteppa) Road Project. Consultant's report. TA 8945-TAJ. Unpublished.

Figure 4: Expected Future Road Network Condition under Different Budget Scenarios

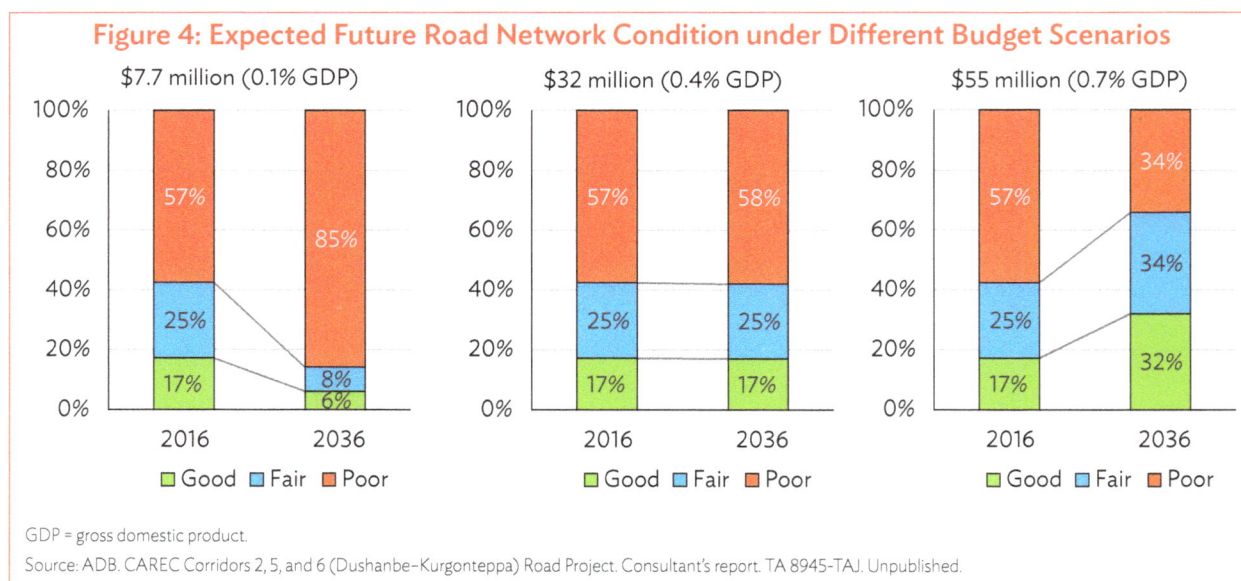

GDP = gross domestic product.

Source: ADB. CAREC Corridors 2, 5, and 6 (Dushanbe–Kurgonteppa) Road Project. Consultant's report. TA 8945-TAJ. Unpublished.

---

30   ADB. CAREC Corridors 2, 5, and 6 (Dushanbe–Kurgonteppa) Road Project. Consultant's report. TA 8945-TAJ. Unpublished.

54.   The Road Fund existed from 1992 to 1999 but was abolished in 2000 to comply with the International Monetary Fund's requirements to consolidate the national budget.[31] Currently, various road user charges are collected but are not allocated specifically to the road subsector's use. The recently approved RAMS Action Program stipulates that a new road maintenance fund is to be established by 2024 to secure road maintenance budgets at a required level.[32] Potential funding sources would be toll revenues and other road user charges.

55.   The government introduced a road user tax as part of the original Road Fund to finance the road subsector.[33] The tax remains as a tax on the gross revenue of corporate taxpayers. The tax rate is 0.25% for trading, procurement, and supply sale activities, and 1% for other activities. The tax rate is regularly reduced and is now planned for abolishment in 2021. In 2019, revenue from the Road User Tax amounted to approximately $38 million. A fuel excise tax of €55 per ton is also collected for petrol (over $0.04/liter), while it is much lower for diesel at €8 per ton (under $0.01/liter). In 2015, the revenue amounted to $15 million with 293 million liters of petrol and 259 million liters of diesel consumed. A vehicle tax is collected by local governments at the time of technical inspection and is differentiated by engine capacity and type of vehicle. In 2018, the total revenue collected from the vehicle tax was approximately $20 million.[34]

56.   Toll collection is only carried out on the road running from Dushanbe via Khujand to the Uzbekistan border (Chanak). The 337 km road[35] is under a 30-year concession contract that started in 2010. Toll rates range from TJS0.2/km for category I vehicles ($0.02/km) to TJS1.9/km for category IV vehicles ($0.20/km).[36] Traffic data published by the MOT for the Anzob tunnel show an average daily traffic volume of 1,000 vehicles per day. Based on this traffic volume, the total toll revenue for all five toll stations is estimated to be $10 million per year (assuming higher traffic volumes around Dushanbe and Khujand), which is equivalent to approximately $26,500/km/year.

57.   Other charges collected from road users include overloading fees and fines and customs duties on imported vehicles. The total amount collected from these sources is estimated to exceed $60 million per year.

Road Asset Management System

58.   The MOT has been working on establishing a road asset management system (RAMS) to improve its capacity for longer-term and evidence-based planning to ensure road operation sustainably. Data were collected, and a Microsoft Access database was prepared in 2008 but is no longer available in the MOT except in printed form. With the support provided under the World Bank-financed Second Phase of the Central Asia Road Links Program,[37] a Trassa survey vehicle was recently procured to collect roughness data. However, the roughness data are not linked to GPS data and can only be exported in PDF file type, making it more suitable for checking completed

[31]   ADB. 2000. *Report and Recommendation of the President to the Board of Directors: Proposed Loan and Technical Assistance Grant to the Republic of Tajikistan for the Road Rehabilitation Project.* Manila; and ADB. 2004. *Project Performance Audit Report for Postconflict Infrastructure Program in Tajikistan.* Manila.

[32]   Government of Tajikistan. 2020. *Road Asset Management System Program for 2021–2024* (Decree No. 706). Dushanbe.

[33]   International Monetary Fund. 1998. *Tajikistan: Recent Economic Developments.* IMF Staff Country Reports Vol. 1988/16. Washington, DC.

[34]   ADB. 2019. *Technical Assistance Consultant's Report: Road Asset Management Road Map.* Manila (TA-8789 REG: CAREC Knowledge Sharing and Services in Transport and Transport Facilitation). https://www.adb.org/sites/default/files/linked-documents/52042-001-sd-02.pdf.

[35]   This excluded road sections through Dushanbe and Khujand as well as the three large tunnels (Dusti, Shahristan, and Anzob).

[36]   The concessionaire's website (Innovative Road Solutions. http://irs.tj/) provides the details of each vehicle category. Category I vehicles are "cars or trucks with cargo loads up to 2 tons. Passenger buses with capacity up to 19 seats." Category II vehicles are "medium-type vehicles with a carrying capacity of cargo from 2 to 7 tons. Passenger buses with capacity from 20 up to 39 seats." Category III vehicles are "large-type vehicles with a carrying capacity of cargo from 7 to 14 tons. Passenger buses with capacity of more than 40 seats." Category IV vehicles are "specialized type vehicles or trucks with carrying capacity of cargo above 14 tons."

[37]   World Bank. 2015. *Project Appraisal Document on a Proposed Credit in the Amount of SDR 26.5 million (US$ 38.25million) and a Proposed Grant in the Amount of SDR 4.7million (US$ 6.75milllion equivalent) to the Republic of Tajikistan for the Second Phase (CARs-2) of the Central Asia Road Links (CARs) Program.* Washington, DC.

construction works but less for network data collection. A road database was also developed with World Bank support, together with a set of algorithms for predicting road deterioration, identifying maintenance needs, and prioritizing budget allocations. However, the different elements of this system are not inter-linked well, and there remain concerns about whether the database has been properly tested and calibrated for actual data. The World Bank has also provided support for the procurement of about 40 traffic counting stations, most of which have been programmed and are operational in different locations around the country. These stations provide full-time traffic counts with data accessible remotely (footnote 37).

59. On 31 December 2020, the government approved the RAMS Action Program through Government decree 706 (footnote 32). This program defines the different actions to be undertaken in 2021–2024, mainly on the following: (i) collecting inventory, condition, and traffic data for the road network under the MOT's jurisdiction; (ii) developing the road database wherein collected data are regularly entered; (iii) improving the data analysis tools and subsequent annual and multiannual evidence-based planning; and (iv) improving road subsector financing through earmarked resources, specifically for road maintenance. In addition, on the same date, the Road and Transport Sector Digitalization Unit was established in the MOT. The unit is dedicated for implementing the RAMS Action Program and operationalizing Tajikistan's RAMS, and has been working on the development of the RAMS database with the support of development partners. Given the unit's growing importance in the road subsector operation, the MOT plans to increase the budget and the number of unit staff. The MOT is forming an RAMS coordination meeting with development partners to achieve the smooth implementation of the action program in a timely manner.

Road Vehicles and Driving License Systems

60. The State Automobile Inspectorate under the Ministry of Internal Affairs is authorized to execute safety controls for ensuring traffic safety and compliance of vehicles with relevant standards. It is responsible for issuing driving licenses and registering vehicles. The number of registered vehicles has been steadily increasing in Tajikistan, with the number of vehicles per 1,000 people doubling since 2000 (Table 19). The vehicle density is the highest in Dushanbe, followed by Sughd Oblast. At 43 vehicles per 1,000 people, the vehicle ownership in Tajikistan is similar to that of Uzbekistan or Afghanistan but lower than those in other countries in the region. The total vehicle fleet is approximately 400,000, of which over 85% are passenger cars and light vehicles, mainly second-hand from Europe, 9% heavier trucks, 4% buses, and 1% motorcycles.

Table 19: Registered Vehicles per 1,000 people

Region	2000	2001	2002	2003	2004	2005	2006	2007	2008	2009	2010	2011	2012	2013	2014	2015	2016	2017	2018
Dushanbe	24	30	27	28	33	27	42	47	47	68	53	54	60	60	66	67	73	69	68
DRS	23	22	20	21	22	23	25	27	33	44	38	38	39	41	41	40	44	39	38
Sughd	28	26	25	25	25	25	29	32	37	55	46	51	53	56	57	56	64	58	58
Khatlon	7	9	10	10	11	11	15	17	21	28	27	26	26	27	28	28	30	29	28
GBAO	15	15	15	15	15	16.8	17	17	20	36	24	25	27	29	34	36	47	38	39
Total	**19**	**19**	**19**	**19**	**20**	**21**	**24**	**26**	**31**	**44**	**38**	**39**	**40**	**42**	**43**	**43**	**48**	**44**	**43**

DRS = Districts of Republican Subordination, GBAO = Gorno–Badakhshan Autonomous Oblast.

Source: Statistics Agency under the President of the Republic of Tajikistan.

61. To obtain driver licenses, people are required to attend specific training courses in authorized educational institutions (public or private). Training courses required depend on the vehicle category (Table 20). A practical examination must be taken after completing the required training courses to demonstrate driving skills at the inspectorate or assigned places.

Table 20: Driving License by Type of Vehicle

Category of Driving License	Type of Vehicles
A	Motorcycles with or without a side trailer with an engine displacement of more than 125 cm³ and a permissible maximum mass not exceeding 400 kg
B	Automobiles (except for category A vehicles) with a permissible maximum mass not exceeding 3,500 kg and the number of seats (in addition to the driver's seat) not exceeding 8 Cars of category B, coupled to a trailer, with a permissible maximum mass not exceeding 750 kg Cars of category B, coupled to a trailer, with a permissible maximum mass exceeding 750 kg, not exceeding the mass of the vehicle without load, and the total permissible maximum mass of such a composition not exceeding 3,500 kg
C	Vehicles, except those that belong to category D, with a permissible maximum mass exceeding 3,500 kg Cars of category C, coupled to trailers, with a permissible maximum mass not exceeding 750 kg
D	Vehicles intended for the carriage of passengers and having more than 8 seats, in addition to the driver's seat Vehicles of category D, coupled to trailers, with a permissible maximum mass not exceeding 750 kg
BE	Vehicles of category B, coupled to trailers, with a permissible maximum mass exceeding 750 kg and exceeding the mass of the vehicle without load Vehicles of category B, coupled to trailers, with a permissible maximum mass exceeding 750 kg and the total permissible maximum mass of such a compound exceeding 3,500 kg
CE	Vehicles of category C, coupled to trailers, with a permissible maximum mass exceeding 750 kg
DE	Vehicles of category D, coupled to trailers, with a permissible maximum mass exceeding 750 kg

cm³ = cubic centimeter, kg = kilogram.

Source: Government of Tajikistan. The Order for Admission to Driving Vehicles (Decree No. 550). Approved on 1 November 2019.

62.   In 1994, the country acceded to the Vienna Convention on Road Traffic, which was agreed upon at the United Nations Economic and Social Council's Conference on Road Traffic in 1968. Since 2014, Tajikistan has issued biometric driving licenses that can be used internationally in more than 200 countries that have adopted the convention (inclusive of the 2006 amendment that came into effect in 2011).

Public Transport Service Operation

63.   Public transport service operation is governed by the various legislative acts and government's relevant resolutions, some of which are related to business activities in the country. Operating transport services in roads, railways, and aviation subsectors requires the purchase of the concerned license in accordance with the Law on Licensing of Selected Activities in the Republic of Tajikistan (No. 37, 2004), and the license must be renewed every 5 years. The license is issued by the State Service for Transport Supervision and Regulation under the MOT (Figure 2, para. 14). Meanwhile, international and domestic transport services (passengers and goods) require another license, following the government decree, "On approval of the Order on the Specifics of Licensing Certain Types of Activities (No. 685 on 31 December 2020)." The license is issued under the MOT after examination by the License Commission. The decree emphasizes the licensee's compliance with safety requirements, technical standards, and regulations as stipulated in the government's relevant decrees and acts.

64.   Private and public transport service operators are active in Tajikistan. Urban public transport service operators are state-owned enterprises and operate mainly intracity services (bus or trolleybuses), while private operators are more involved in providing international transportation of goods and passengers. Some of the private operators offer intercity services by car (taxi) as well.

Road Safety

65.   The State Automobile Inspectorate reported 1,212 road traffic accidents and 391 fatalities[38] in 2019, or 4.2 fatalities per 100,000 people (Table 21). International roads are responsible for a third of the accidents and fatalities. The World Health Organization estimates the number of fatalities to be 3–4 times higher than those reported by the government and the number of fatalities in 2016 to be 1,577, or 18.1 per 100,000 people. As shown in Table 22, this is similar to Kazakhstan, the Russian Federation, and the PRC but higher than other countries in the region. Vehicle drivers (22%) and passengers (36%) account for about half of the fatalities, but most fatalities involve pedestrians (40%) and cyclists fatality is low at 2%. Major behavioral risk factors for road crashes identified in Tajikistan include drunk driving, nonuse of helmets, nonuse of seat belts or child restraint, and speeding.[39]

Table 21: Road Accidents and Fatalities

Indicator	Accidents					Fatalities				
	2015	2016	2017	2018	2019	2015	2016	2017	2018	2019
International	527	485	467	482	368	245	211	230	190	137
Republican	121	120	96	131	105	18	34	36	48	91
Urban	827	721	740	672	739	170	182	167	157	163
Total	1,475	1,326	1,303	1,285	1,212	433	427	433	395	391
Per 100,000 people	17.4	15.3	14.7	14.1	13.0	5.3	4.9	4.9	4.3	4.2

Note: Road accident data for the local roads are not available.

Source: Government of Tajikistan, Ministry of Transport.

Table 22: Road Traffic Accident Fatalities, 2016

Indicator	TAJ	UZB	KAZ	KGZ	RUS	TKM	AFG	PRC	PAK
Reported fatalities	427	2,496	2,625	812	20,308	543	1,565	58,022	4,448
WHO estimated fatalities	1,557	3,617	3,158	916	25,969	823	5,230	256,180	27,582
Fatalities per 100,000 people	18.1	11.5	17.6	15.4	18.0	14.5	15.1	18.2	14.3

AFG = Afghanistan, KAZ = Kazakhstan, KGZ = Kyrgyz Republic, PAK = Pakistan, PRC = People's Republic of China, RUS = Russian Federation, TAJ = Tajikistan, TKM = Turkmenistan, UZB = Uzbekistan, WHO = World Health Organization.

Source: WHO. 2018. *Global Status Report on Road Safety*. Geneva.

66.   As shown in Table 21, the number of accidents and fatalities reduced in 2015–2019, particularly on international roads. This reduction could be partly attributed to recent road safety initiatives, which have been introduced in the country's road development projects. Development partners have been encouraging the country to incorporate road safety features in road designs as well as launching road safety awareness campaigns. In 2016, Tajikistan, together with the other CAREC member countries, endorsed the CAREC Road Safety Strategy up to 2030.[40]

67.   Further efforts to improve road safety are required for republican and urban roads. Although the number of accidents on republican roads has remained more or less constant, the number of fatalities has increased nearly fivefold in the past 5 years. More accidents and fatalities tend to occur in urban areas.

68.   Accidents and fatalities incur a high cost on the economy. McMahon and Dahdah (2008)[41] estimate that the costs of a road accident fatality are equivalent to approximately 70 times the GDP per capita. If we

---

[38]   Reported as dead within 7 days of the accident.

[39]   World Bank. 2020. *Guide for Road Safety Opportunities and Challenges: Low- and Middle-Income Country Profiles*. Washington, DC.

[40]   ADB. 2017. *Safely Connected: A Regional Road Safety Strategy for CAREC Countries, 2017–2030*. Manila.

[41]   K. McMahon and S. Dahdah. 2008. *The True Cost of Road Crashes: Valuing Life and the Cost of a Serious Injury*. Basingstoke: International Road Assessment Programme.

apply this to Tajikistan, the cost of one fatality is estimated at $62,338 when using the 2019 GDP per capita of $890.54 (footnote 4). The cost of a serious injury is estimated at 25% of the cost of a fatality, or $15,585. Assuming that there are 10 serious injuries per fatality following McMahon and Dahdah (2008), the cost of road accidents would be estimated at $85.3 million per year based on the government-reported fatalities, or $339.7 million per year based on the World Health Organization-estimated number of fatalities.

Climate Change

69. Tajikistan is a country prone to natural disasters, with floods, avalanches, mudflows, and landslides, and they cause not only traffic disruption but also significant economic loss.[42] These disasters, resulting from high seasonal precipitation and annual snowmelt, are further exacerbated by the steep topography and related high runoff speeds and slope instability. Over 500 km of the roads under the MOT's jurisdiction are exposed to such adverse natural events.[43] Natural events weaken roads and their associated infrastructure such as bridges, drainage systems, and other supporting structures, causing significant damages and making them impassable and/or unsafe. Climate change is expected to manifest itself in Tajikistan in increased temperatures as well as increased precipitation intensities and extreme weather events, especially in spring and summer.[44] Another concern is the changes in flows of rivers and groundwater.[45] The high temperature causes risks of deformation of road pavements, deterioration of the subbase, and thermal expansion of bridge joints. To avoid such risks, the government prohibits heavy vehicles of more than 6 tons from driving between 10 a.m. and 8 p.m. during summer when the temperature exceeds 26°C. Such traffic disruptions will increase if temperatures continue to rise. The expected precipitation intensities, together with increased snowmelt, will increase water levels and rainfall runoff volumes and speeds, affecting road foundations and causing subsequent floods, erosion, mudflows, and landslides. Improving the drainage system and strengthening bridges are suggested to cope with the larger runoff volumes, as well as carrying out slope stabilization works to mitigate landslide risks.

Planned Investments

70. The NTDPTS focuses on the rehabilitation and upgrade of 2,240 km of international roads and 1,760 km of republican roads. The total estimated budget requirement is $816 million, and the estimated allocation to the international road networks is almost double compared with the amount for the national roads (Table 23). Although the budget for international roads remains almost constant in each period, the budget for republican roads is set to gradually increase. This implies the importance of developing the republican road network, which is in line with one NTDPTS's priority of ensuring people's all-year access throughout the country.

Table 23: Planned International and Republican Road Investments, 2011–2025

Indicator	2011–2015	2016–2020	2021–2025	Total
Length (kilometer)	**711.8**	**1,337.2**	**1,954.4**	**4,003.4**
International	609.3	739.0	893.1	2,241.4
Republican	102.5	598.2	1,061.3	1,762.0
Cost ($ million)	**211.7**	**233.7**	**370.9**	**816.3**
International	193.9	153.4	190.7	538.0
Republican	17.8	80.3	180.2	278.3

Source: National Target Development Program for the Transport Sector of the Republic of Tajikistan up to 2025.

---

[42] World Bank. 2021. *Assessment of Economic Impacts from Disasters Along Key Corridors*. Washington, DC.

[43] Deutsche Gesellschaft für Internationale Zusammenarbeit. 2020. *Climate Change Profile: Tajikistan*. Dushanbe.

[44] World Bank. 2013. *Tajikistan: Overview of Climate Change Activities*. Washington, DC.

[45] United Nations Environment Programme. 2015. Tajikistan Climate Facts and Policy: Policies and Processes. https://wedocs.unep.org/bitstream/handle/20.500.11822/9861/-Tajikistan_climate_facts_and_policy_policies_and_processes-2015country_scorecards_for_climate_policy_Tajikistan.pdf.pdf?sequence=3&isAllowed=y.

71.   The program also lists investments for constructing or rehabilitating bridges including nearly 600 bridges with a combined length of 5.1 km and a budget requirement of around $20 million (Table 24).

Table 24: Planned Bridge Investments, 2011–2025

Indicator	2011–2015	2016–2020	2021–2025	Total
Bridges (no.)	166	173	237	576
Length (meter)	1,330	2,052	1,720	5,102
Cost ($ million)	8.1	6.6	5.5	20.2

Source: National Target Development Program for the Transport Sector of the Republic of Tajikistan up to 2025.

3.3 Rail Subsector

72.   Railways are generally suited for the transport of bulky and heavy goods over long distances. They carry a significant volume of international freight to and from Tajikistan, as examined in section 3.1.[46]

Railway Infrastructure

73.   Of the total railway network of 975 km, only 28.4 km is double track. None of the tracks are electrified. The main line has a length of 692 km, with 216 km of track at stations and 67 km of access spurs. Spread over the network are 33 stations. Tajikistan Railways owns 47 locomotives, 400 passenger cars, and 1,982 freight wagons. The average age of passenger cars is 35 years, compared to 30 years for freight wagons.

74.   The track is broad gauge (1,520 millimeters), the same as those in other countries of the Commonwealth of Independent States, facilitating rail travel with and through neighboring countries. However, access to seaports and important import and export markets in the PRC, Iran, or Turkey requires a change in gauge since these countries mainly use standard gauge (1,435 millimeters).

75.   Most of the railway lines in Tajikistan were built in the Soviet era. These lines were an integral part of the railway system of the Soviet Union, with borders between the Soviet republics being irrelevant for network planning. The breakup of the Soviet Union resulted in three isolated sections of railway track (northern, central, and southern), each connected to the Uzbekistan railway network.

76.   Map 4 shows Tajikistan's railway network. The northern line runs from Bekobod in Uzbekistan to Khujand and onto the town of Konibodom and further to Kokand in eastern Uzbekistan. There is an additional line running south from Konibodom to Isfara. The northern line used to carry two-thirds of all rail traffic in Tajikistan, mainly catering to transit traffic between two parts of Uzbekistan. However, in 2016, Uzbekistan constructed an alternative path within its territory to develop the new route without crossing the border with Tajikistan. This led to a drop in traffic on the northern line, with total freight volume decreasing by 25% and freight turnover dropping by nearly 50% from 2015 to 2017. However, the northern line remains an essential link serving the northern part of Tajikistan. In September 2020, the Protocol of the Intergovernmental Commission on Trade and Economic Cooperation was signed between Tajikistan and Uzbekistan, under which the transit function of the northern network is expected to be resumed in 2021.[47]

77.   The central line runs from Samarkand in Uzbekistan to Tursunzoda, where the Tajikistan Aluminum Company is located, and Dushanbe.

---

[46] This section is developed based on ADB. 2021. *Railway Sector Assessment for Tajikistan.* Manila. The supplementary information collection was carried out by the TA consultants in 2020–2021, with assistance from Tajikistan Railways and the MOT.

[47] The Bekobod–Istiklol section is expected to resume in 2021 for freight transportation.

Map 4: Railway Network in Tajikistan

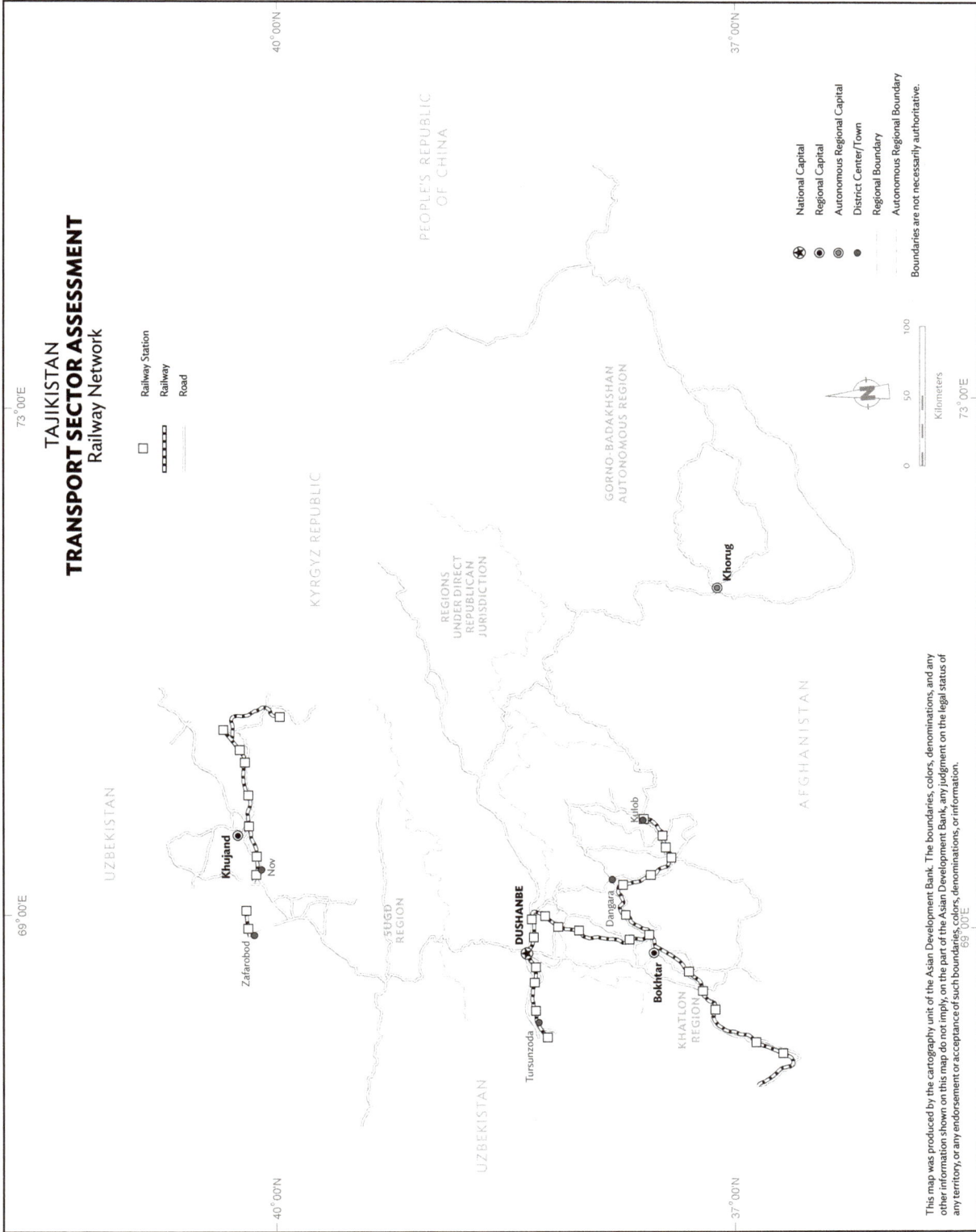

TAJIKISTAN
TRANSPORT SECTOR ASSESSMENT
Railway Network

□ Railway Station
▭▭▭ Railway
——— Road

UZBEKISTAN

KYRGYZ REPUBLIC

SUGD REGION

Zafarobod
Khujand
Nov

Tursunzoda
DUSHANBE
Dangara
Bokhtar
KHATLON REGION

Kulob

REGIONS UNDER DIRECT REPUBLICAN JURISDICTION

GORNO-BADAKHSHAN AUTONOMOUS REGION

Khorug

PEOPLE'S REPUBLIC OF CHINA

AFGHANISTAN

UZBEKISTAN

69°00'E   73°00'E

40°00'N

37°00'N

⊛ National Capital
◉ Regional Capital
◎ Autonomous Regional Capital
● District Center/Town
—·—· Regional Boundary
———— Autonomous Regional Boundary
Boundaries are not necessarily authoritative.

N

0   50   100
Kilometers

This map was produced by the cartography unit of the Asian Development Bank. The boundaries, colors, denominations, and any other information shown on this map do not imply, on the part of the Asian Development Bank, any judgment on the legal status of any territory, or any endorsement or acceptance of such boundaries, colors, denominations, or information.

Source: Asian Development Bank.

78.   The southern line runs from Termez in Uzbekistan to Aiwanj, Shakhrituz, and Bokhtar. The line was extended by 132 km from Bokhtar to Kulob in 1999.

79.   In 2016, the central and southern lines were connected through the construction of the section of track between Dushanbe and Bokhtar, with support from the PRC. This section has made it possible to travel on rail between the two major cities without passing through Uzbekistan.

80.   All international railway transport requires crossing through Uzbekistan, the only country with rail connections through four border crossings. Tajikistan Railways, therefore, remains very dependent on access to the rail network in Uzbekistan to connect to other countries and between its northern and central-southern railway lines. Connectivity of the southern railway line to Uzbekistan was restricted between 2011 and 2017 mainly because a bridge on the Galaba–Amuzang section was destroyed, making the route nonoperational. In March 2018, this constraint was lifted, coinciding with improved bilateral relations between Uzbekistan and Tajikistan. However, there remain hindrances for Tajik transporters and traders to use railways to access to the port in Bandar Abbas (para. 25), and they tend to use roads.

81.   Track maintenance is lacking, and much of the network is in poor condition. This results in frequent derailments and low speeds averaging 30–40 km/hour, which is less than half of the maximum speed of freight and passenger trains at 80 km/hour. Tajikistan Railways is keen to replace railway sleepers and add ballast to improve the condition of the network.

Passenger Services

82.   Tajikistan Railways runs international passenger trains from Dushanbe, Kulob, and Khujand to Moscow (Table 25). Domestic trains operate once a week between Dushanbe and Khujand (through Uzbekistan) and twice a week between Dushanbe and Kulob via Bokhtar. There is also a daily suburban train between Dushanbe and Tursunzoda.

Table 25: Passenger Train Services

International	Trips/Week	Domestic	Trips/Week
Dushanbe–Moscow	3	Dushanbe–Bokhtar–Kulob	2
Kulob–Moscow	1	Dushanbe–Tursunzoda	7
Khujand–Moscow	1		
Dushanbe–Khujand (via Uzbekistan)	1		

Source: Tajikistan Railways.

83.   Passenger traffic makes up a tiny part of Tajikistan Railways operations, but the number of passengers is steadily increasing by approximately 5% per year. Passenger turnover, expressed in passenger-km, has been increasing at a higher rate by an average of 19% per year since 2015, suggesting that passengers' travel distances have become longer. Considering the destinations of the available railway services as shown in Table 25, the number of passengers heading to Moscow may have been increasing. Furthermore, most passengers are likely seasonal migrant workers residing in large cities such as Moscow and providing remittances to their families.[48] As their remittances account for more than 30% of the country's GDP (para. 28), the railways to and from Moscow play an essential role in Tajikistan's economy. Table 26 shows the total rail passenger volume and turnover during 2014–2020.

---

[48]   J. Schottenfeld. 2017. *The Midnight Train to Moscow*. https://foreignpolicy.com/2017/08/10/the-midnight-train-to-moscow-tajikistan-migration/ (accessed 20 October 2021).

Table 26: Rail Passenger Volume and Turnover

Indicator	2014	2015	2016	2017	2018	2019	2020 (Jan–Nov)
Passenger volume ('000)	449.3	424.9	452.1	530.6	545.3	416.8	416.8
Passenger turnover (million passenger-km)	17.5	16.0	18.4	27.9	33.1	28.1	20.1

km = kilometer.

Source: Tajikistan Railways.

Freight Services

84.　　Tajikistan Railways is primarily a freight transport operation entity, with freight trains making up approximately 95% of its traffic. Freight volumes continuously dropped between 2014 and 2017, which could be attributed to the loss of transit traffic over the northern line with the construction of the alternative route within Uzbekistan (Table 27).[49] The same trends were observed in the freight turnover in ton-km, largely due to complications observed in rail travel to Turkey, Europe, and the deep seaports. This issue has resulted in a shift toward road transport, which is more flexible in the routes. Both freight volumes and turnover have bounced back since 2018, likely because the border crossing between Tajikistan and Uzbekistan became operational. Nonetheless, the overall share of railway transport remains marginal.[50]

Table 27: Rail Freight Volume and Turnover

Indicator	2014	2015	2016	2017	2018	2019
Freight volume (ton '000)	6,808.6	6,125.6	5,454.2	4,646.5	5,348.3	5,798.9
Freight turnover (million ton-km)	391.0	316.9	228.3	165.1	223.6	231.7

km = kilometer.

Source: Tajikistan Railways.

85.　　Since its network is fragmented and located only in the west of the country, Tajikistan Railways cannot provide an important transit function or easily respond to domestic transport needs, and its role is largely limited to import and export traffic. With regard to domestic freight transport, railways are responsible for only 0.5% of the total freight transport in tonnage. In terms of international freight traffic, railway transport remains dominant, with 77.0% of all international freight transport being carried by rail in tonnage (Table 5), although this has been dropping steadily in favor of road transport. International rail freight transport forms 98.1% of total rail freight in tonnage.

86.　　Tajikistan Railways faces ever-increasing competition with road transport. With improving road conditions and direct routes to Afghanistan, the Kyrgyz Republic, and the PRC, road transport can lower costs. Tajikistan Railways must compete with many domestic and foreign truck operators operating in a very competitive market. Many foreign truck operators are willing to offer discounted prices to cover the costs of the return journey. While these truck operators use the road network that is maintained and improved using government funding, Tajikistan Railways must cover the costs of maintaining the railway network itself. The low profit margins make it difficult to secure the required investments in railway infrastructure and rolling stock.

---

[49]　Freight traders of consumables and oil or chemical materials who worked between Tashkent and the Fergana and Namangan regions used the northern line in Tajikistan. However, after the Angren–Pap railway line in Uzbekistan was opened in 2016 by Uzbekistan Railway, those freight traders likely have used the new line.

[50]　ADB. 2021. *Railway Sector Assessment for Tajikistan.* Manila.

87.   A market analysis carried out as part of the ADB Railway Sector Assessment for Tajikistan in 2021 (footnote 50) reveals that railway transport was preferred for oversized cargo, bulk cargo (alumina, cement, coal, minerals), petroleum products, and chemicals. This was due to the easy processing and the relative safety of railway transport. Road transport was preferred in the case of consumer products, time-sensitive cargo, high-value goods, and perishable goods. Road transport is generally faster, more reliable, and can provide a door-to-door service.

88.   Rail containerization is poor as most freight transport makes use of closed wagons. Of 2,058 freight wagons owned by Tajikistan Railways, only 143 flat wagons are suitable for container transport. Tajikistan Railways has some 100 containers only (footnote 50). Container cranes of Tajikistan Railways are also often nonoperational, slowing down containerization. The volume of container transport varies widely over the years. The volume of inbound container transport is much higher than that of outbound transport, requiring the transport of empty containers and increasing transport costs (para. 32) (Table 28).

Table 28: Loaded Containers Transported by Rail
('000 ton)

Loaded Containers	2014	2015	2016	2017	2018
Inbound	59.6	30.5	26.2	22.1	37.5
Outbound	2.3	1.5	1.0	0.7	0.6
Total	**61.9**	**32.0**	**27.2**	**22.8**	**38.1**

Source: ADB. 2021. *Railway Sector Assessment for Tajikistan*. Manila.

State Unitary Enterprise Tajikistan Railways

89.   The railway network in Tajikistan was built during the Soviet era and the Central Asia Railway, headquartered in Tashkent, was responsible for its operation. After the independence, the railway in the territory was taken over by the SUE Tajikistan Railways (*Rohi Ohani Tajikistan*), which was established by Decree No. 244 in 1995. Tajikistan Railways is a state-owned commercial unitary enterprise established to provide freight and passenger transport services to and from Tajikistan in a profitable manner. Tajikistan Railways is a natural monopoly in the rail subsector and is regulated in accordance with Article 5 of the Law on Natural Monopolies. As of January 2021, Tajikistan Railways has 5,074 staff who are responsible for (i) preparing timetables for train operations in coordination with neighboring countries; (ii) managing the use of the rolling stock; (iii) overseeing the maintenance, repair, and replacement of railway track and rolling stock; and (iv) constructing associated facilities along the railway networks owned by the Tajikistan Railways. The Construction Directorate in Tajikistan Railways is responsible for constructing new railway lines. Under Tajikistan Railways are joint stock companies and unitary enterprises involved in freight marketing (JSC Logistics and Procurement Service), passenger services (UE Musofirbari), and railway construction (UE Rohsoz). OJSC Railway Freight Dispatch is currently an independent entity, with 100% of shares belonging to the government. However, it works with Tajikistan Railways based on an agreement between the two entities and practically remains part of the Tajikistan Railways structure (Figure 5).

Figure 5: Organizational Structure of Tajikistan Railways

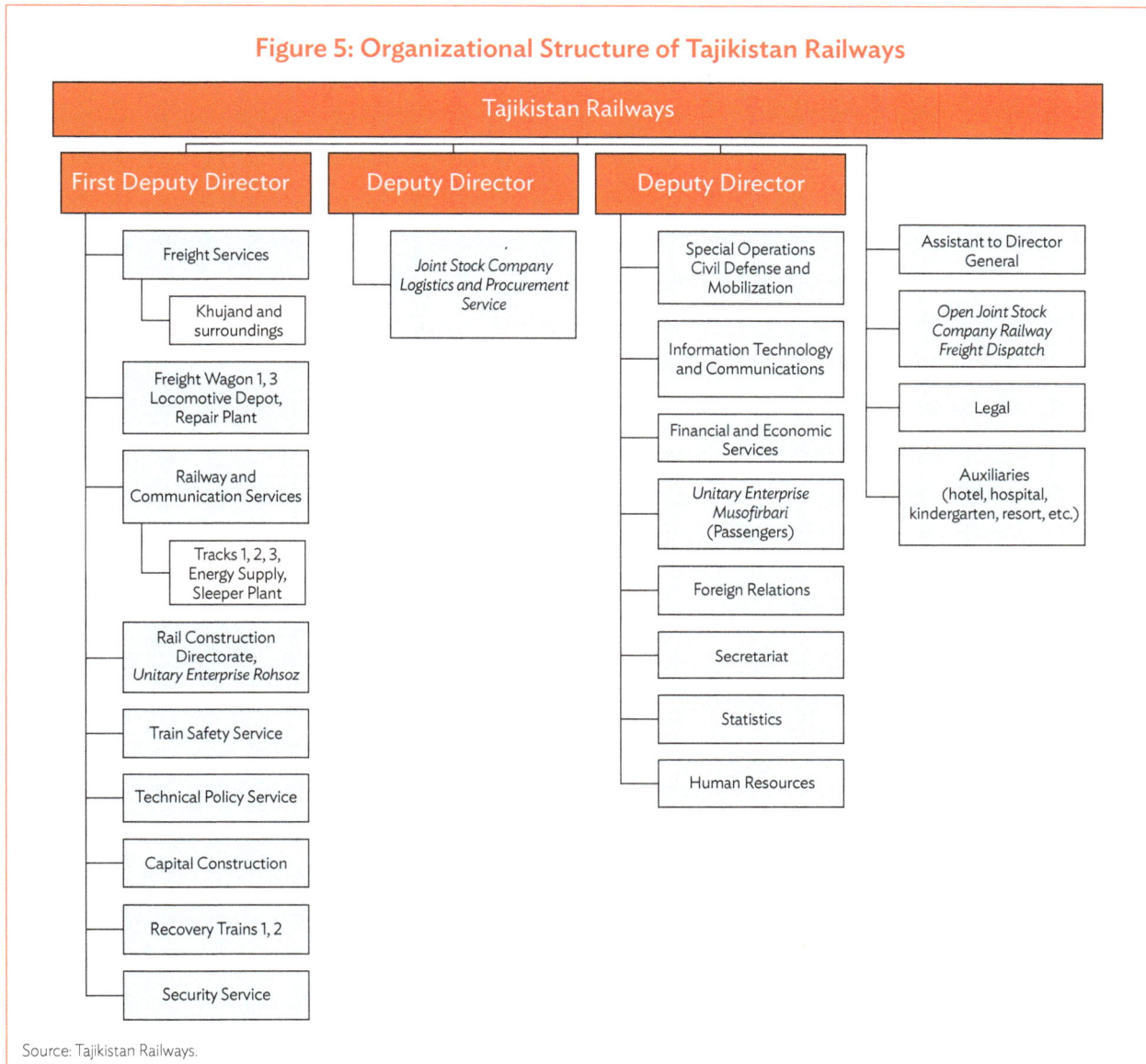

Source: Tajikistan Railways.

90.   Tajikistan Railways has consistently achieved a profit. Even when the transit revenue of the northern railway line has been reduced since 2016 due to the loss of transit traffic (footnote 49), it managed to reduce expenditure to maintain a profit. This is likely achieved by deferring maintenance, repairs, and replacements to future years. Tajikistan Railways develops a maintenance strategy of the existing railway lines, and maintenance works are carried out according to the strategy to ensure that the existing railway lines and associated facilities keep properly operational in the long run, as Tajikistan Railways intends to expand the railway network.

Table 29: Revenue and Expenses of Tajikistan Railways
(TJS million)

Indicator	2014	2015	2016	2017	2018	2019	2020 (Jan–Nov)
Revenue	334.7	321.2	319.3	354.9	391.1	487.1	492.9
Expense	338.4	294.6	295.6	319.4	380.1	446.7	455.5
Profit for SUE	-	**21.6**	**23.3**	**30.3**	**29.9**	**30.3**	**36.5**
Profit margin (%)	-	8.3	7.3	8.5	7.6	6.2	7.4

SUE = state unitary enterprise.

Source: Tajikistan Railways.

91. At the same time, employee numbers in Tajikistan Railways are very high in relation to the passenger and freight turnover, as evidenced by the ratio (0.05) of passenger and freight turnover per employee for Tajikistan Railways (Figure 6). This indicates a need for improving its operational efficiency.

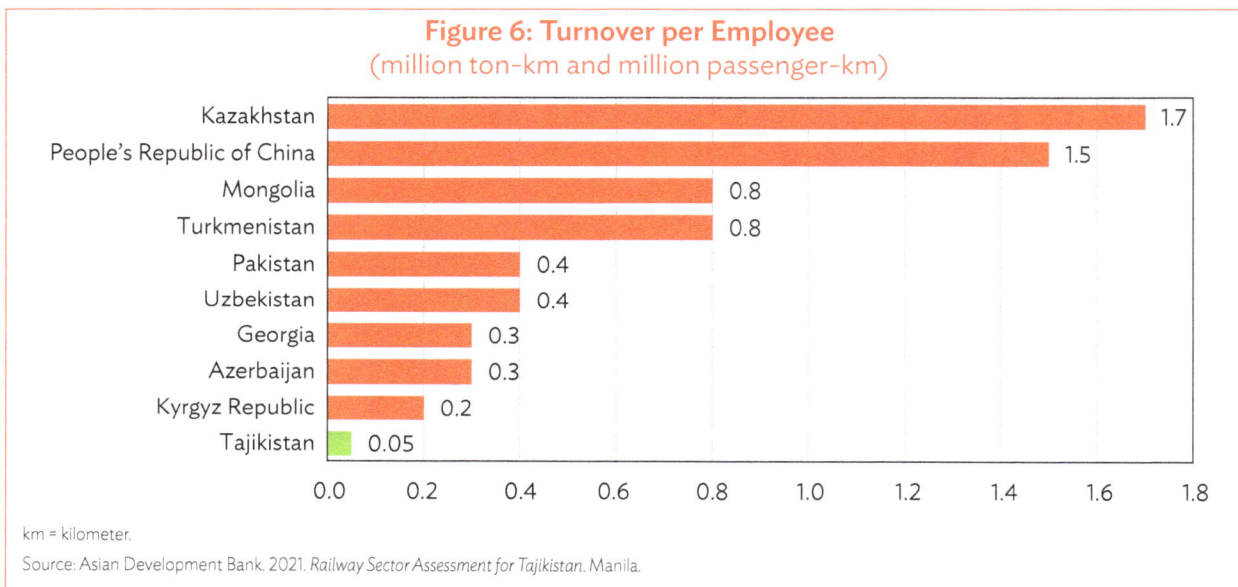

Figure 6: Turnover per Employee
(million ton-km and million passenger-km)

km = kilometer.

Source: Asian Development Bank. 2021. *Railway Sector Assessment for Tajikistan*. Manila.

92. Tajikistan Railways is not resourced enough to carry out marketing activities, identify business needs, attract the interests of freight traders, and improve the service quality. More specifically, there are reports of quotations taking a long time to prepare, payments for shipments being required to be made in advance, or track-and-trace services not being provided. No staff are specifically assigned to sales and marketing. Out of 5,047 staff, only three staff set tariffs. The OJSC Railway Freight Dispatch is in charge of the marketing and sale of freight transport based on an agreement with Tajikistan Railways. Meanwhile, for passenger transport, the Unitary Passenger Transport Enterprise manages the marketing and sales of tickets.

93. Tariffs for railway transport service are subject to review by the Antimonopoly Commission, and Tajikistan Railways needs the commission's review and approval for adopting new tariffs to their services. The review is carried out annually; hence tariffs to be newly introduced may not always reflect the real market conditions. The approval process for new tariffs causes a lag between the need for a price change and the actual price change. This procedural requirement reduces flexibilities in tariff setting by Tajikistan Railways. The result is that prices do not consider the latest market conditions, with little flexibility to increase tariffs where possible (bulk

goods and liquids) and decrease tariffs where competition is high. In addition, the costs of international railway transport are largely out of Tajikistan Railways' hands, with tariffs for the use of foreign railways set by the countries concerned. These current situations around tariff setting make it hard for Tajikistan Railways to have a competitive pricing policy and compete with road freight transport, which is currently not subject to such tariff control.

94.   Passenger and freight turnovers achieved by Tajikistan Railways are low, even when considering the limited size of the railway network. A comparison in Figure 7 shows a turnover density[51] of only 0.38, the lowest in the region.

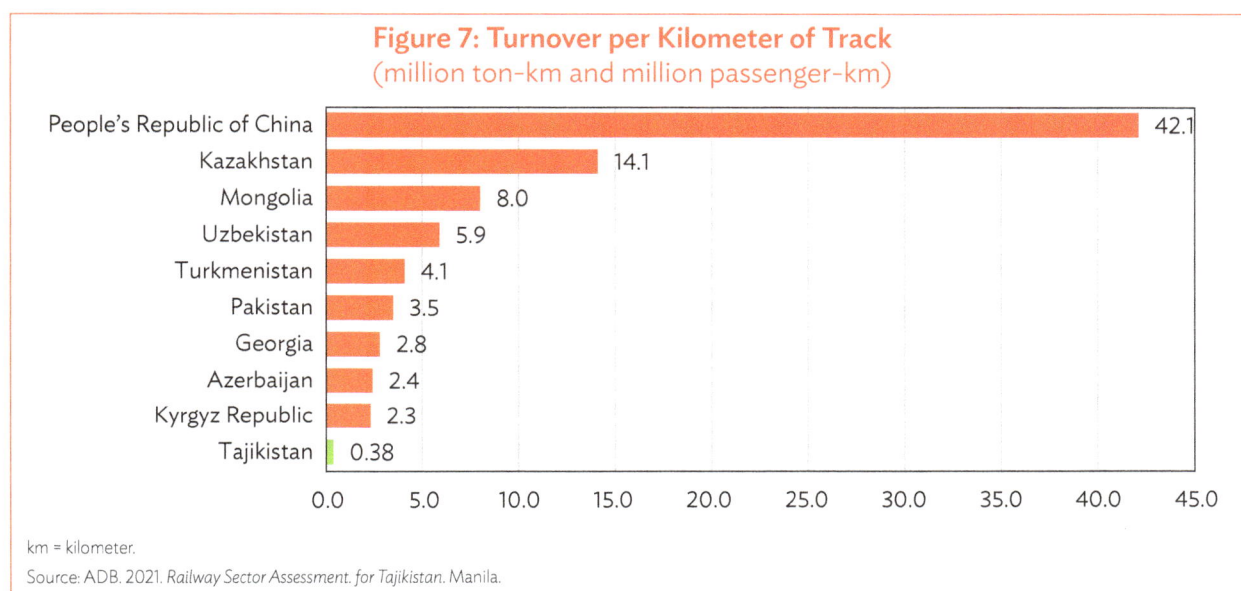

Figure 7: Turnover per Kilometer of Track
(million ton-km and million passenger-km)

People's Republic of China	42.1
Kazakhstan	14.1
Mongolia	8.0
Uzbekistan	5.9
Turkmenistan	4.1
Pakistan	3.5
Georgia	2.8
Azerbaijan	2.4
Kyrgyz Republic	2.3
Tajikistan	0.38

km = kilometer.

Source: ADB. 2021. *Railway Sector Assessment. for Tajikistan*. Manila.

95.   Tajikistan Railways limits itself to railway transport and does not support arranging road or shipping transport linkages to offer a door-to-door transport service. Tajikistan Railways has sold off some of its multimodal terminals and rails spurs, making it even more difficult to provide a door-to-door service. Some sections of spur lines have been sold to different parties, significantly complicating the use of these spurs and requiring coordination with and payments to several parties. Supporting the construction of spur lines to connect to major shippers could also make railway transport more attractive.

96.   Tajikistan Railways needs to collect commercial metrics, carry out regular market analyses, and further focus on developing and nurturing relationships with existing and potential users. In doing so, it needs to focus on enhancing its strengths as a long-distance transporter of bulk goods and liquids with quicker processing at border crossings and improving its door-to-door service. Such reform will likely require significant restructuring. To materialize this, in addition to the above physical investment, Tajikistan Railways needs to be reformed into a more commercially oriented entity. One possible option is to change this SUE into an OJSC.

Planned Investments

97.   The NTDPTS focuses on replacing sleepers, ballast, and worn-out tracks on existing lines; repairing and reconstructing bridges; improving repair shops; and purchasing new rolling stock. It also proposes to develop feasibility studies for new lines connecting (i) Kolkhozabad (Jaloliddin Balkhi) to the border with Afghanistan

---

[51]   Turnover density is the sum of the passenger turnover (passenger-km) and freight turnover (ton-km) divided by the length of the track (a track length of 682 km is used here).

at Panji Poyon (50 km), (ii) Vakhdat to the border with the Kyrgyz Republic at Karamyk (296 km), and (iii) the North–South line connecting the northern and central/southern sections of the railway network. Tajikistan Railways finances investments in rolling stock and existing railway line repairs and maintenance.

98.   During this assessment, Tajikistan Railways informed the following areas for future investments to enhance profitability and operational efficiency, as well as improve service quality: (i) construction of the new railway line connecting to Panji Poyon linking to Afghanistan; (ii) electrification of sections of the northern line (Bekobod–Istiklol), the central line (Kuduli–Dushanbe–Vakhdat), and the southern line (Amuzang–Bokhtar–Kulob); (iii) development of a centralized dispatch center and automatization of technical operations; (iv) development of a high-speed rail network on the lines Dushanbe–Tursunzoda and Dushanbe–Bokhtar–Kulob to reduce passenger travel times to the capital; (v) procurement of rolling stock including locomotives, passenger wagons, and freight wagons; and (vi) development of a network of terminals and logistic centers along the railway network to support door-to-door services. These areas would require substantial investments, and feasibility studies are suggested to be conducted to confirm their financial and operational viability. Such feasibility studies may need to capture the latest travel patterns and requirements, which may have changed due to the coronavirus disease (COVID-19).

99.   Specifically, new routes through Afghanistan can indeed improve access to seaports, Turkey, and Europe. Discussions have been ongoing about the construction of a 51 km railway line from Kolkhozabad (Jaloliddin Balkhi) to the border with Afghanistan at Panji Poyon, together with a 65 km railway line in Afghanistan to connect Sher Khan Bandar to Kunduz and Mazar-e-Sharif. The investment is estimated at $130 million and aims to enhance the efficiency of the railway network in Tajikistan and the connectivity with Afghanistan and its surrounding countries. However, the feasibility of this connection needs to be reassessed in light of the resumed railway traffic between Tajikistan and southern Uzbekistan. This connection may achieve additional benefits if the railway line in Afghanistan is extended westward to connect to Herat, with onward connections to Iran and the deep seaport of Bandar Abbas. Uzbekistan and Afghanistan agreed in December 2017 to build a new 760 km railroad between Mazar-e-Sharif and Herat at an estimated cost of $1.8 billion.[52] There is also a proposal to extend a railway line from Mazar-e-Sharif southward, connecting to Torkham and the railway network in Pakistan to access the deep seaport in Karachi and eventually Gwadar.

3.4 Aviation Subsector

100.   Tajikistan's aviation subsector was liberalized in 2008 with support from the World Bank,[53] splitting up the state-owned Tajik State Air that included the national airline Tajik Air, the operation of airports, and air traffic control. The liberalization introduced a separation of functions among the regulator Civil Aviation Agency (CAA), different airports, air traffic control, and airlines, each at arm's length from the government. The CAA under the government currently carries out policy implementation, regulation, and planning in the aviation subsector. The CAA is responsible for developing the subsector's relevant policies, which the government will consider and adopt. In the process, the MOT may participate and provide suggestions, but the CAA is independent of the MOT. The four international airports are currently managed by respective OJSCs, operating commercially. SUE Tajik Air

---

[52]   Strategy for the Development of the Transport System of the Republic of Uzbekistan until 2035. Draft. https://regulation.gov.uz/ru/document/3867.

[53]   World Bank. 2010. *Implementation Completion and Results Report (IDA Grant Nos. H246, H325 and H451) on Grants in the Amount of SDR 7.0 million ($10.0 Million Equivalent); SDR 6.7 million ($10.0 Million Equivalent); and SDR 13.3 million ($20.0 Million Equivalent) to the Republic of Tajikistan for the Programmatic Development Policy Operations.* Washington, DC; and World Bank. 2014. *Implementation Completion and Results Report (IDA Grant Nos. H246, H325, and H451) on Grants in the Amount of SDR 16.9 million ($25.4 Million Equivalent); SDR 6.4 million ($10 Million Equivalent); and SDR 13.2 million ($20 Million Equivalent) to the Republic of Tajikistan for the Programmatic Development Policy Operations.* Washington, DC. Support was provided under a series of the World Bank-financed six Programmatic Development Policy Grant Projects (2006–2013).

Navigation supervises air traffic control. Two domestic airlines and approximately 15 foreign airlines operate flight services. However, in 2018, the operation of airports and navigation was transferred to the CAA.

Civil Aviation Agency

101.   The CAA was established under the Air Code of Tajikistan (Law 116, 2005 with latest amendments in Law 1315, 2016) with the transformation of the Department for Civil Aviation under the MOT into an independent agency. The Regulations for the CAA (Decree No. 596, 2017) define the responsibilities of the CAA as implementing the state aviation policy, developing plans and programs, organizing the use of the airspace, developing common standards, certifying and licensing for civil aviation, analyzing the aviation subsector in Tajikistan, and monitoring tariffs and fees.

102.   The policy-setting function was originally anticipated to be executed by the MOT, including setting policies for the sector, signing bilateral and multilateral agreements, regulating tariffs, and dealing with other policy matters. However, the MOT has no department or staff dedicated to the aviation subsector. In practice, policies are prepared by the CAA and submitted to the government for approval.

103.   The CAA has 6 departments with 38 staff positions. The Oversight Department is responsible for supervising the operation of the airports and air traffic control, aviation security, and flight operations (Figure 8). The Regulation and Standards Department is responsible for the technical regulation of flights and licensing airports and air traffic control. The Aviation Incident Investigation Commission, initially with the Department for Civil Aviation under the MOT, is headed by the director of the CAA.

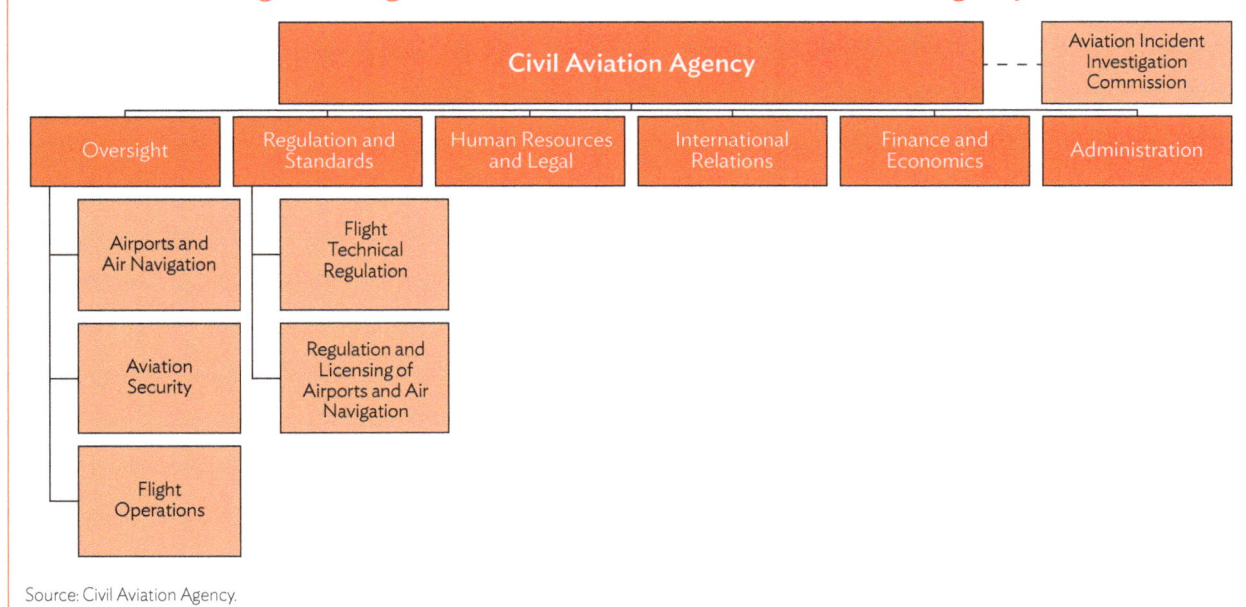

Figure 8: Organizational Structure of the Civil Aviation Agency

Source: Civil Aviation Agency.

104.   In 2018, the management of four international airports was transferred from the MOT to the CAA. The CAA is now responsible for setting and implementing the subsector's policies and regulating the airport companies, air navigation enterprises, and airline companies.

Airports

105.   Tajikistan has two main international airports in Dushanbe and Khujand and two smaller international airports in Bokhtar and Kulob (Map 1 and Table 30). These four airports served 2,245,200 passengers in 2019, an increase of 12% compared to 2018. As shown in Figure 9, Dushanbe International Airport served 63% of these passengers (1,422,000), with Khujand International Airport in the north of the country serving 30% (664,900 passengers). Kulob International Airport is served almost exclusively by Ural Air and had 102,200 passengers (5%), while Bokhtar International Airport is served by Nordwind Airlines and had 55,900 passengers (2%). Khorug Airport in the eastern region is the other domestic airport with scheduled flights by Tajik Air. Dushanbe and Khujand airports also serve as domestic airports, with flights between Dushanbe and Khujand and between Dushanbe and Khorug. There are several other domestic airports, but these do not have scheduled flights and only have occasional seasonal flights or charter flights.

Table 30: Main Airports in Tajikistan

Location	IATA	ICAO	Airport Type	Airlines
Dushanbe	DYU	UTDD	International	Somon Air, Tajik Air, Air Astana, Avia Traffic Company, China Southern Airlines, flydubai, Iran Aseman Airlines, Kam Air, S7 Airlines, SCAT Airlines, Turkish Airlines, Ural Airlines, Utair, Uzbekistan Airways
Khujand	LBD	UTDL	International	Somon Air, Tajik Air, China Southern Airlines, Nordwind Airlines, S7 Airlines, SCAT Airlines, Ural Airlines, Utair
Kulob	TJU	UTDK	International	Ural Airlines
Bokhtar	KQT	UTDT	International	Nordwind Airlines
Khorug	...	UTOD	Domestic	Tajik Air

... = data not available, IATA = International Air Transport Association, ICAO = International Civil Aviation Organization.

Source: Technical assistance consultant.

Figure 9: Passenger Traffic by Airport, 2019
(%)

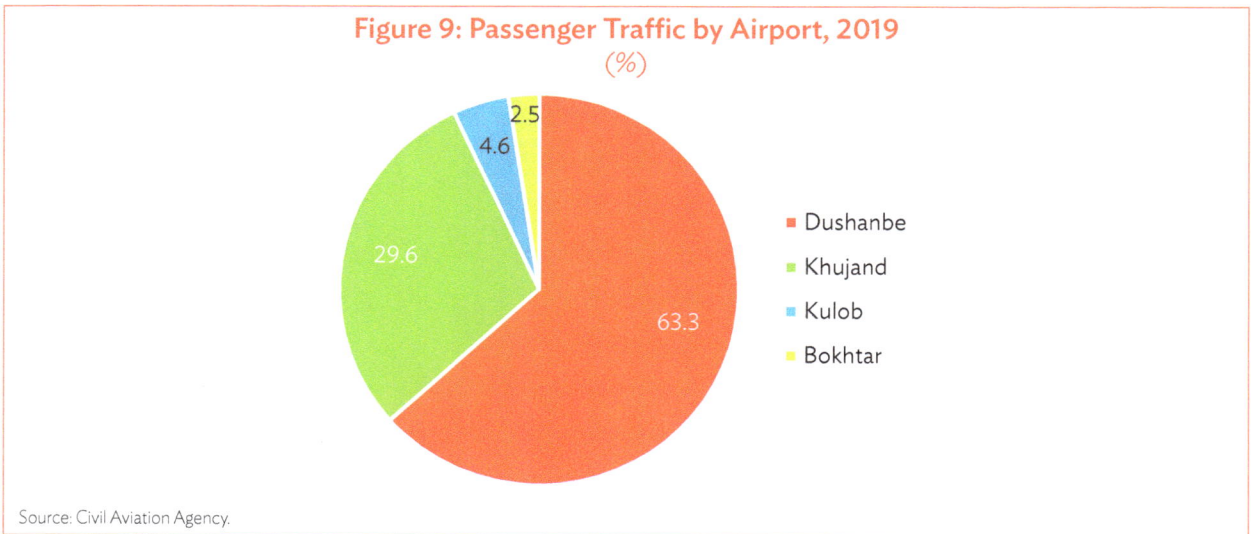

- Dushanbe 63.3
- Khujand 29.6
- Kulob 4.6
- Bokhtar 2.5

Source: Civil Aviation Agency.

106.   The government has been improving several airports. At Dushanbe International Airport, the runway was lengthened and improved in 2005 by the French Air Force and can serve the largest planes and loads. A new international passenger terminal was recently constructed with a $26.5 million loan from France, capable of serving 500 passengers per hour. A new cargo terminal is under construction, and air navigation equipment has been improved with a $20.4 million grant from the Japan International Cooperation Agency. At Khujand International Airport, air navigation equipment is being modernized with a $3.9 million loan from the EBRD complemented by $4.7 million government financing.

107.   The airports in Dushanbe and Khujand are the farthest apart (300 km, 5 hours by road). The Dushanbe Airport serves a market in central and southern Tajikistan, while the Khujand Airport for the northern region, and the airports have significant numbers of passengers (over 0.5 million passengers per year). The two airports in Bokhtar and Kulob are close to Dushanbe (2–3 hours by road) and each other (2 hours). They likely serve the same market (southern Tajikistan) and compete for the same passengers, resulting in small passenger numbers (50,000–100,000). To attract airlines and passengers, these airports are reducing charges to airlines for using the airport and their associated services.

108.   The four international airports used to form a part of the SUE Tajik Air, but Decree No. 491 of 2008 split them off as separate SUE under the State Committee for Investments and State Property Management. Subsequently, Decree No. 707 of 2009 defined that an OJSC would be established for operating each international airport, and the OJSCs would be under the jurisdiction of the MOT. Khorug Airport is operated under the OJSC Dushanbe International Airport and receives subsidies from the OJSC. After the creation of the CAA, the management of the four international airports was transferred from the MOT to the CAA under Regulation 536 of 2018. Other domestic airports are under the control of local authorities but do not have scheduled flights.

109.   The international airports operate as independent commercial enterprises and are in direct competition with each other. Some international airports like Bokhtar and Kulob have lowered their service charges to attract low-cost airlines like Ural Airlines and Nordwind Airlines. However, this comes at the expense of the other airports in Khujand and Dushanbe. The operation of multiple airports might decrease operational revenues in each airport as sharing the limited demand among the airports consequently reduces the profitability of individual airports (para. 107). The government is planning to construct a new international airport in Dangara, which would result in competition with the existing three international airports in Bokhtar, Dushanbe, and Kulob and eventually lower financial and operational efficiencies of those three airports. Further, there is road and railway connectivity in the region (to Dushanbe, from Kulob it is 200 km and 3–4 hours by road, while it is about 100 km and 2 hours by road from Bokhtar and Dangara). With the low passenger numbers in Bokhtar and Kulob airports (approximately 150,000 passengers per year for both), the rationale of having three international airports less than 100 km apart and within the same region needs to be reexamined. On the other hand, the eastern region of Tajikistan is served only by Khorug Airport.

Airlines

110.   Domestic flights are primarily between Dushanbe and Khujand,[54] although the number of flights is being reduced with the improvement of roads and the construction of three tunnels between Dushanbe and Khujand, assuring year-round access. Khorug is the only other domestic airport with scheduled flights from Dushanbe. Domestic flights are popular in the winter when the roads become impassable due to snowfall and avalanches.

111.   Tajikistan has liberalized its air traffic rights and currently has international flights to 11 countries[55] operated by 2 domestic airlines and approximately 15 foreign airlines. Most of these flights route to one or two destinations in those countries. However, for the Russian Federation, the flights route to 18 destinations, reflecting the importance of the Russian Federation for migrant workers from Tajikistan. These workers tend to return to Tajikistan in the winter when construction work in the Russian Federation slows down. With remittance income forming approximately one-third of the GDP and over half of rural households depending on remittances as their main source of income, these flights are essential to the economy, similar to international railways (paras. 28 and 83).

---

[54]   In 2011, 89% of the domestic flights in Tajikistan was for the Dushanbe–Khujand route (footnote 7).

[55]   The 11 countries include Afghanistan, Germany, India, Iran, Kazakhstan, the Kyrgyz Republic, the PRC, the Russian Federation, the United Arab Emirates, Turkey, and Uzbekistan.

112.   Tajikistan has two domestic airlines, Somon Air and Tajik Air. Approximately one-third of the air passengers are carried by domestic airlines, particularly Somon Air. Tajik Air was the national airline of the former Tajik Soviet Socialist Republic and responsible for air traffic control and airport operation, but these functions were put under separate state-owned companies in 2008. Tajik Air continued to be state-owned and was transformed into an OJSC under the MOT in 2009 (Decree No. 707) and transferred to the CAA in 2018 (Decree No. 536). It now operates six aircraft (Boeing 757 and Boeing 737, two Antonov AN-28 propeller planes, and two Mil MI-8 helicopters). It operates flights from Dushanbe to Bishkek, Almaty, Tehran, Delhi, Urumqi, and five destinations in the Russian Federation, as well as domestic flights between Dushanbe and Khujand or Khorug. Before the liberalization of the sector, Tajik Air had certain privileges such as not being charged for airport operations and air traffic control and receiving preferential treatments compared with other airlines, as the same company carried out these operations. Since the liberalization, Tajik Air has been exposed to competition with private airline companies including Somon Air. Tajik Air has faced financial problems and has been receiving the government's support including deferment of tax payments. As part of state support, a comprehensive reform of the company is planned. Somon Air is a private company created in 2008 that operates six aircraft (two Boeing 737-900, two Boeing 737-800, and two Boeing 737-300). It operates flights from Dushanbe and Khujand to Frankfurt, Delhi, Almaty, Dubai, Istanbul, Tashkent, Urumqi, 12 locations in the Russian Federation, and domestic flights between Dushanbe and Khujand.

113.   Tajikistan is further served by approximately 15 international airlines. The Russian low-cost Ural Airlines, S7 Airlines, and Nordwind Airlines are the most active, serving multiple destinations and different airports in Tajikistan. Turkish Airlines and China Southern Airlines provide regular international flights to and from Dushanbe. Most flights operate only a few days a week, and many are seasonal. As per the CAA, based on the data in 2020, the international airlines operate up to 80% of the flights and carry approximately two-thirds of air passengers.

Air Traffic Control

114.   Air traffic control is managed by the SUE Tajik Air Navigation (Tajik Aero Navigatsiya), which was created under the MOT by Decree No. 491 in 2008, splitting it off from the state-owned company Tajikistan State Air. In 2018, it was transferred to the CAA by Decree No. 536. Apart from the main office in Dushanbe, it has branch offices in Khujand, Kulob, and Bokhtar and has a service office in Khorug. As per the Safety Audit Results in 2016 by the International Civil Aviation Organization, the country's rating was relatively lower than the global average on licensing, operations, air navigation services, and airdromes.[56]

115.   Tajikistan airspace has 35 air corridors, which are managed by Tajik Air Navigation, including 26 crossings into Uzbekistan airspace, 5 into the Kyrgyz Republic, and 4 into Afghanistan. In 2019, Tajik Air Navigation provided services for a total of 46,000 flights. Aircraft are charged with fixed rates depending on the size of the aircraft and its flight path. The rates are set and collected directly by Tajik Air Navigation. The revenue is used to provide services and procure and maintain equipment.

116.   Tajik Air Navigation is currently receiving technical support from the EBRD[57] in improving its air navigation equipment. The project of $9.2 million, including a loan of $7 million, aims to install air navigation and meteorological equipment in the airports of Dushanbe and Khujand. This assistance is expected to strengthen the air navigation services, which require strengthening as per the International Civil Aviation Organization's safety audit (footnote 56).

---

[56]   International Civil Aviation Organization. Safety Audit Results: UNOAP Interactive Viewer. https://www.icao.int/safety/pages/usoap-results.aspx (accessed 20 October 2021).

[57]   EBRD. 2019. Tajikistan Air Navigation (https://www.ebrd.com/work-with-us/projects/psd/tajikistan-air-navigation.html).

Planned Investments

117.   The National Development Strategy of the Republic of Tajikistan for the Period up to 2030 (footnote 8) speaks of connecting the different regions in Tajikistan by air, although this has not yet materialized. The development of airports and flights is very much oriented toward international flights, and most of these flights have destinations in the Russian Federation. Domestic flights are restricted to Dushanbe–Khujand, with limited flights between Dushanbe and Khorug. Such a limited domestic flight operation reflects improved road conditions and the construction of tunnels that allow roads to remain open throughout the winter season. It also reflects the limited viability of such flights, which would need to be subsidized to make them financially viable and affordable for local people.

118.   Meanwhile, the NTDPTS presents a plan of improving the existing infrastructure and strengthening the subsector operation. Some were completed, such as the construction of the new international terminal in Dushanbe, the ongoing improvement of the air navigation equipment of Tajik Air Navigation, and the subsector's institutional reform and commercialization. Further planned investments include Bokhtar International Airport (flight control center and airport reconstruction), Kulob International Airport (taxiway), Dushanbe International Airport (second runway), and domestic airports (rehabilitation for use by small aircraft).

119.   The MOT proposes investments in airports that include the rehabilitation of Khujand International Airport ($11.7 million), Bokhtar International Airport ($57.5 million), and the domestic Panjakent Airport in the center-west of the country near the Uzbekistan border ($5.2 million).[58] The government is also planning to construct a new international airport in Dangara (para. 109). Although the Khatlon Oblast is the most populous region with more than one-third of Tajikistan's population (footnote 23), it already has two international airports with very limited passenger numbers.

120.   In addition, the CAA expects various investments in the subsector, including the construction of transit terminal(s) or expansion/rehabilitation of other facilities in the existing airports, mainly Dushanbe and Khujand, in line with the government's objective of creating a regional transit hub.[59] However, several larger cities in Central Asia are expected to serve as regional aviation hubs, such as Almaty and Tashkent. Any airport in Tajikistan would face intense competition.

121.   To ensure optimal use of available resources for the subsector's development, the government should carefully review and analyze potential investments for financial and operational viability, as well as compatibility among individual initiatives. Interdependencies between investments in individual airports should be mapped out to better understand the impact of an investment in one airport on the financial viability of other airports. In undertaking further analysis, the impacts of the COVID-19 pandemic on people's travel behavior in Tajikistan and surrounding countries must be considered.

3.5 Cross-Border and Logistics Facilitation

122.   Border crossing points (BCPs) and logistics centers perform an essential role in the transport of goods and passengers across borders and the transshipment of goods between and within different transport modes. The health of Tajikistan's economy rests heavily on efficient BCPs and logistics, as it is a landlocked country.

---

[58]   MOT. Perspective Projects for Civil Aviation Sector. https://www.mintrans.tj/en/civil-aviation/perspective (accessed 20 October 2021).

[59]   During the interviews, the CAA proposed the following: (i) improving navigation and lighting equipment in Kulob Airport, Bokhtar International Airport, and Khorug Airport; (ii) renewing the 15-year-old runway pavement in Dushanbe; and (iii) constructing a freight terminal in Khujand Airport.

Border Crossing Points

123.   There are 16 main BCPs, most of which are connected by international roads (Table 31 and Map 5). The BCPs at Dusti and Fotehobod with Uzbekistan, Guliston with the Kyrgyz Republic, and Panji Poyon with Afghanistan are the most important for road transport, as they serve large truck volumes of more than 10,000 trucks per year. The road BCPs in Patar (Konibodom) with the Fergana Valley region of Uzbekistan and Kulma with the PRC serve smaller truck volumes of up to 5,000 trucks per year. Other road BCPs serve mainly passenger cars and only a small number of trucks. The roads connecting the BCPs in Guliston and Patar (Konibodom) do not form part of the CAREC corridors or Asian highways, despite being responsible for approximately 20% of international truck traffic. With the World Bank's support, the roads connecting to Guliston and Patar (Konibodom) BCPs have been recently upgraded. The Guliston BCP is essential because the Jirgatol BCP is currently a bilateral border crossing between Tajikistan and the Kyrgyz Republic and does not allow travelers and traders to and from other countries. Therefore, travelers and traders from the PRC to Tajikistan (and vice versa) must use either the Guliston BCP, resulting in a longer distance, or the Kulma BCP with a long mountainous road through Khorug, which is in poor condition and is often closed in winter. Opening the Jirgatol BCP to third countries will likely reduce international truck transport through Guliston BCP.

Table 31: Main Border Crossing Points

#	BCP	Country	Road	Rail	Vehicles/Year	% Trucks
1	Aiwanj	Uzbekistan (Gulbahor)	IR11	Southern	-	
2	Dusti	Uzbekistan (Sariosiyo)	IR02	Central	10,000–20,000	>95
3	Sarazm	Uzbekistan (Jartepa)	IR13		5,000–10,000	10
4	Zafarobod	Uzbekistan (Havastobod)	IR15		2,500–5,000	<5
5	Hashtyak	Uzbekistan (Bekobod)	RR091	Northern	2,500–5,000	<5
6	Fotehobod	Uzbekistan (Oybek)	IR01		10,000–20,000	>95
7	Navbunyod	Uzbekistan (Pap)	IR19		2,500–5,000	10
8	Patar (Konibodom)	Uzbekistan (Andarkhon)	IR14	Northern	2,500–5,000	>95
9	Ravot (Konibodom)	Uzbekistan (Ravot)	RR070		2,500–5,000	30
10	Guliston	Kyrgyz Republic (Batken)	IR16		10,000–20,000	>95
11	Madaniyat	Kyrgyz Republic (Kairagach)	IR12		-	
12	Jirgatol	Kyrgyz Republic (Karamyk)	IR07		2,500–5,000	<5
13	Kyzylart	Kyrgyz Republic (Bardoba)	IR05		-	
14	Kulma	People's Republic of China (Karasu)	IR04		2,500–5,000	>95
15	Ishkoshim	Afghanistan (Eshkashim)	IR04		-	
16	Panji Poyon	Afghanistan (Sher Khan Bandar)	IR09		10,000–20,000	>95

BCP = border crossing point, IR = international road, RR = republican road.

Source: Government of Tajikistan, Ministry of Transport; and technical assistance consultant.

124.   In addition to the road BCPs, there are four rail BCPs, of which the most important are Dusti BCP on the central-southern network and Bekobod BCP on the northern network. Patar (Konibodom) BCP used to be vital for transit traffic between Tashkent and the Fergana Valley region of Uzbekistan but is now important only for international trade between Tajikistan and the Fergana Valley region. Patar (Konibodom) BCP is becoming more important as transit traffic resumes under the new Protocol of the Intergovernmental Commission on Trade and Economic Cooperation signed between Tajikistan and Uzbekistan (para. 76). The railway between Konibodom BCP and Hashtyak BCP continues to form a part of CAREC corridor 2. The southern crossing between Aiwanj and Termez is not well used because Turkmenistan has closed its borders to transport operators from Tajikistan and international railway transport is oriented northward.

Map 5: Main Border Crossing Points

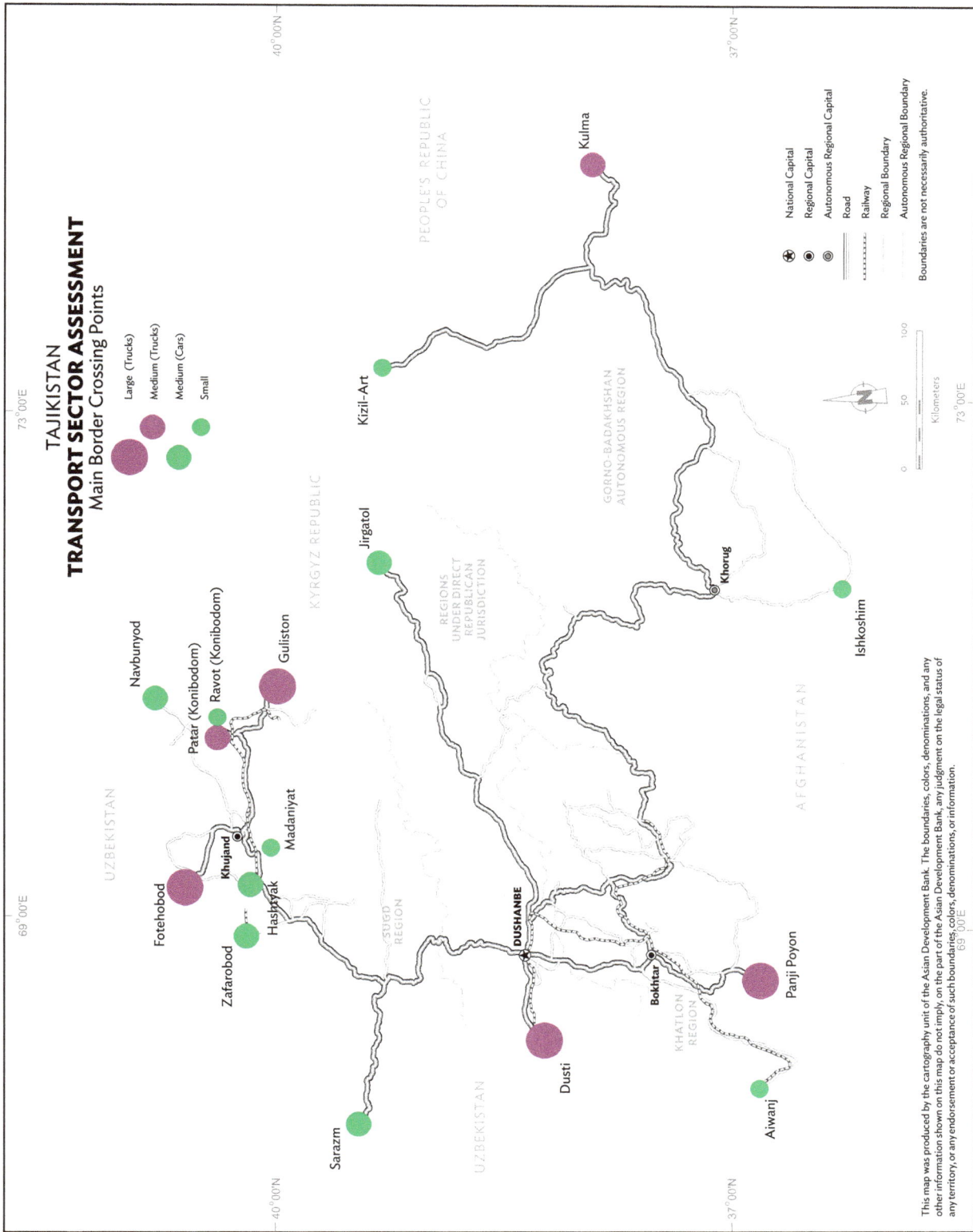

TAJIKISTAN
TRANSPORT SECTOR ASSESSMENT
Main Border Crossing Points

Large (Trucks)
Medium (Trucks)
Medium (Cars)
Small

Kulma

PEOPLE'S REPUBLIC OF CHINA

Kizil-Art

KYRGYZ REPUBLIC

Jirgatol

Navbunyod

Patar (Konibodom)
Ravot (Konibodom)
Guliston

REGIONS UNDER DIRECT REPUBLICAN JURISDICTION

GORNO-BADAKHSHAN AUTONOMOUS REGION

Khorug

Ishkoshim

UZBEKISTAN

Fotehobod
Khujand
Madaniyat
Zafarobod
Hashtyak

AFGHANISTAN

SUGD REGION

DUSHANBE

Bokhtar
Panji Poyon

Dusti

KHATLON REGION

UZBEKISTAN

Sarazm

Aiwanj

National Capital
Regional Capital
Autonomous Regional Capital
Road
Railway
Regional Boundary
Autonomous Regional Boundary

Boundaries are not necessarily authoritative.

N

0   50   100
Kilometers

This map was produced by the cartography unit of the Asian Development Bank. The boundaries, colors, denominations, and any other information shown on this map do not imply, on the part of the Asian Development Bank, any judgment on the legal status of any territory, or any endorsement or acceptance of such boundaries, colors, denominations, or information.

Source: Asian Development Bank.

210017H 20TAJ ABV

125.   Roads connecting to many of the main BCPs have been improved recently, resulting in speed without delays increasing significantly in the CAREC countries. In Tajikistan, the average speed without delays on CAREC corridors is currently just under 40 km/h.[60] However, speed with delays (SWD) has either remained the same or decreased. SWD has dropped from 23.1 km/h in 2017 to 22.5 km/h in 2019. Stagnant or decreasing SWD indicates issues with border crossings and transshipments, which have not improved in line with the infrastructure improvements. Notable in this respect are the BCPs with Afghanistan between Panji Poyon and Sher Khan Bandar and with Uzbekistan between Dusti and Sariosiyo. Table 32 shows that crossing times through the BCPs with both countries require more than 20 hours. In Tursunzoda, the processing time is quite long for traffic from Tajikistan into Uzbekistan, also averaging more than 20 hours, while traffic into Tajikistan only requires an average of fewer than 8 hours. During this assessment, the customs service under the Government of Tajikistan informed its observation that the crossing duration were recently improved. Meanwhile, costs are very high on the border with Afghanistan and for inbound traffic at the Fotehobod BCP with Uzbekistan, averaging $450–$500 per truck. The high BCP costs in Panji Poyon are further increased by the need to change trucks, with BCP costs and other fees making up 55% of the total transport costs for a container shipment from Pakistan to Tajikistan.

Table 32: Average Crossing Duration and Cost for Main Border Crossing Points, 2019

Border Crossing (Tajikistan BCP—Other BCP)	Direction of trade	Tajikistan BCP		Other BCP		Both BCPs	
		Duration (hour)	Cost ($)	Duration (hour)	Cost ($)	Duration (hour)	Cost ($)
Tursunzoda (Dusti)–Sariosiyo	TAJ-UZB	11.0	108	10.1	...	21.1	108*
	UZB-TAJ	3.2	96	4.6	101	7.8	197
Fotehobod–Oybek**	TAJ-UZB	1.4	27	2.8	32	4.2	59
	UZB-TAJ	7.0	360	5.0	15	12.0	375
Isfara (Guliston)–Batken (Kyzylbel)	TAJ-KGZ	0.9	29	0.9	23	1.8	52
	KGZ-TAJ	0.6	21	0.5	13	1.1	34
Jirgatol–Karamyk	TAJ-KGZ	1.2	37	0.6	19	1.8	56
	KGZ-TAJ	0.6	26	2.1	45	2.7	71
Kulma–Karasu	TAJ-PRC	...	...	...	...	...	...
	PRC-TAJ	3.0	91	4.1	207	7.1	298
Panji Poyon–Sher Khan Bandar	TAJ-AFG	3.8	61	20.0	392	23.8	453
	AFG-TAJ	7.2	183	14.2	331	21.4	514

... = data not available.

AFG = Afghanistan, BCP = border crossing point, KGZ = Kyrgyz Republic, PRC = People's Republic of China, TAJ = Tajikistan, UZB = Uzbekistan.

* Only the cost for inbound is counted because of data availability.

** Due to the data availability for 2019, the 2018 data is referred.

Source: ADB. 2020. *CAREC Corridor Performance Measurement and Monitoring: Annual Report 2019.* Manila.

126.   One of the main advantages of railway transport for international shipments is that Tajikistan Railways has a good relationship with customs and can pass the border with Uzbekistan relatively quickly (footnote 50). Where the average time required for crossing the border was 3.8 hours for road transport in 2018, it was only 2.3 hours for railway transport. The BCP cost for railway transport is approximately two-thirds or less of the cost for road transport.

127.   The poor performance of BCPs is also shown in the World Bank's Logistics Performance Index, where Tajikistan ranks 134th out of 167 countries, with an overall score of 2.34 (Figure 10). In the region, only Afghanistan scores worse. In terms of competence and quality of logistics services, Tajikistan scores better than the Kyrgyz Republic, Turkmenistan, and Afghanistan, ranking 132nd, while it ranks 154th in terms of the efficiency of customs

---

[60]   ADB. 2020. *CAREC Corridor Performance Measurement and Monitoring: Annual Report 2019.* Manila.

clearance. The national single window system was launched in 2020 under an ADB-financed project,[61] which is expected to improve the existing BCPs' performance.

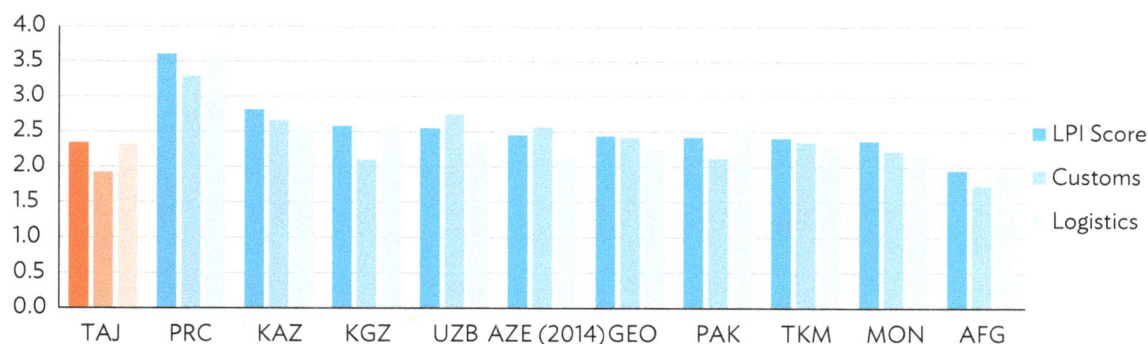

Figure 10: Logistics Performance Index, 2018

AFG = Afghanistan, AZE = Azerbaijan, GEO = Georgia, KAZ = Kazakhstan, KGZ = Kyrgyz Republic, MON = Mongolia, PAK = Pakistan, PRC = People's Republic of China, TAJ = Tajikistan, TKM = Turkmenistan, UZB = Uzbekistan.

Note: The information in 2014 was the latest available information for Azerbaijan.

Source: World Bank, Logistics Performance Index (Country Score Card). https://lpi.worldbank.org/international/scorecard/line/254/C/TJK/2018. (accessed 20 October 2021)

Logistics Centers

128.   Tajikistan has logistics centers in Dushanbe and Khujand that facilitate transshipment between roads and railways within the cities. One of the centers is in Vakhdat, near Dushanbe, which is connected to road and rail infrastructure. Vakhdat lies at the crossroads for routes to Afghanistan, the PRC, and the Kyrgyz Republic. Meanwhile, in Tursunzoda on the border with Uzbekistan, a logistics center was recently constructed, served by both road and rail infrastructure. Following the recent bilateral agreement with Uzbekistan (para. 76), the importance of improving the BCPs along the border with Uzbekistan is growing.

Planned Investments

129.   The NTDPTS foresees the development of logistics centers in regional and district centers, as well as international logistics centers in Vakhdat, Khujand, and Panji Poyon (estimated cost of $1.5 million). Border terminals are also to be constructed (estimated cost of $15 million).

130.   Several potential locations for logistic centers in Tajikistan respond to the continuous growth of trade with the neighboring countries. One is at the border with Afghanistan. Currently, railway transport may be used down to Kolkhozabad, from where transshipment to road is required to reach Panji Poyon on the border with Afghanistan. If the planned railway construction from Kolkhozabad to Panji Poyon (para. 99) is materialized, the transshipment would be required at the border. A logistics center could be suggested along the railway line for facilitating transshipments between rail and road, as well as connectivity west to Uzbekistan or north toward Dushanbe and beyond. The locations could be Kolkhozabad, Bokhtar, or Panji Poyon. Jirgatol on the Dushanbe–Karamyk road near the border with the Kyrgyz Republic is also a possible key location for a logistics center. Although the border crossing does not record high truck traffic, this route has recently been upgraded and forms an alternative connection to the PRC through Sarytash and Irkeshtam in the Kyrgyz Republic. Once the BCP is opened to third countries, this route will likely become much busier.

---

[61]   ADB. 2013. *Report and Recommendation of the President to the Board of Directors: Proposed Loan and Grant to the Kyrgyz Republic and the Republic of Tajikistan for Central Asia Regional Economic Cooperation Regional Improvement of Border Services Project.* Manila.

4. Core Sector Issues and Ways Forward

131.	This chapter summarizes the issues identified in the previous chapters and presents possible actions to facilitate the transport sector's further development in Tajikistan.

132.	**Transition to a strategic and comprehensive approach to transport sector planning.** Tajikistan relies on transport infrastructure largely built during the Soviet era, although there have been drastic geopolitical changes since its independence in 1991. The transport sector is fully acknowledged as a key driver for the country's social and economic development. However, it has not fully performed its expected role. Tajikistan's transport sector must transform itself to accommodate updated needs of the country, whether in terms of the technical requirements of infrastructure or operation and management systems. Tajikistan currently aims to serve a transit function in Central Asia for tourism and trade, but available resources are far more limited against the required investments.

133.	For optimal use of the limited available resources, the government should have a national long-term spatial development program, illustrating (i) economic centers that the government wants to strengthen from their strategic perspective and (ii) physical links among those centers that facilitate trades among them and with the neighboring countries. Each center should be given development strategies, showing how the center and adjoining areas would be developed and which sectors would be drivers for their growth. The links would form one infrastructure network assisting in materializing the strategies of each center and promoting spill-over effects toward surrounding areas. The network comprising those economic centers and links would become the platform for the country's economic growth, which would be prioritized when allocating resources for investments. To enable optimal resource use, the government should also fit its institutional setup to capture the country's long-term needs and reflect periodically on the resource allocation plan. For this, it is considered to be essential to assess the progress of investments under the NTDPTS and derive lessons from their implementation, which should be reflected to the future transport sector program.

134.	Currently, the MOT is responsible for planning roads and railways subsectors, and partially for cross-border and logistics facilities. There is no department responsible for civil aviation subsector in the MOT. Each subsector agency has its own investment plan which at times seems to operate independently of other subsector plans. The MOT should develop a comprehensive sector program in close coordination with key subsector agencies such as Tajikistan Railways, CAA, and Customs Service, as well as other government agencies. The program must ensure alignment with the country's development strategies, particularly those related to economic development, as well as the said national long-term spatial development plan. The MOT should carry out travel and trade demand forecasts incorporating a scenario analysis at the national and regional levels. Such quantitative analyses will enhance the reliability of the sector program and enable the MOT to review and update the projection periodically to determine their investment plans. In addition, the approach to look at Tajikistan's transport development as a whole at the national and regional levels will allow the government to prioritize the development of BCPs and multimodal logistic centers, which are becoming critical for the country's economic growth and relationships with the neighboring countries. Moreover, it is suggested that the MOT and relevant subsector agencies jointly define functions of each subsector for the country's economic development. This may resolve potential overlaps of investments in the subsectors along the arterial corridors and contribute to efficient resource allocation in transport sector.

135.   **Deliver a structured capacity development program.** The government should strengthen the sector's institutional capacity as a whole to implement the future transport sector program as formulated and periodically monitor, review, and assess implementation progress. It is suggested that the government undertake a comprehensive assessment of transport sector agencies and their human resource competency to identify gaps against the ones required for executing the program and design a structured capacity development program. The structured program will contribute to filling the gaps as well as helping the future staff implement the transport sector program including the program's continuous evolvement.

136.   **Sustain efforts on road maintenance and asset management.** Recent progressive improvement of the international and national road network requires the government's attention to their maintenance, however this assessment confirmed that road maintenance budgets from the government are chronically insufficient. This long-lasting issue has led to the deterioration of roads, despite the continuous financial assistance from development partners. The country's road subsector must be adjusted to the current road assets' status. To solve this immediate issue, the MOT should implement the action plan enclosed in the RAMS Action Program, which was adopted as a government decree in December 2020 (para. 59). In particular, the government should establish a road maintenance fund by 2024 to ensure dedicated funds are available for maintaining the country's roads. The MOT should work closely with the Ministry of Finance and other authorities. Equal attention should also be paid to local roads that are under the local governments' jurisdiction. Local authorities chronically encounter insufficiency in their maintenance budgets and receive subsidies from the national government to provide the maintenance to their responsible roads (para. 44). To ensure that local roads will receive maintenance as necessary, it is suggested that local roads will be integrated in the MOT's RAMS and their maintenance budgets will be covered under the road maintenance fund. Furthermore, for implementing the RAMS Action Program properly, it is essential that MOT will have dedicated staff trained on operating and managing the RAMS for roads under its jurisdiction and the trained staff would share their experience and technical expertise with local governments in managing roads under their responsibility.

137.   **Provide all-weather roads providing last-mile connectivity for all.** This action is in line with the NTDPTS. In recent decades, priority has been given to developing the international highway networks (CAREC corridors and Asian highways). On the other hand, most republican roads and local roads remain deteriorated with substandard maintenance works. Such roads tend to be in remote and mountainous or geographically challenging areas, which are often disaster-prone and left behind economically. People living in such areas have suffered from seasonal road closures, isolating them from their full participation in social and economic activities and expanding socioeconomic disparities across the country. The government's focus is now moving from the investment of international road networks to that of republican and local roads. Given the limited resources, the government needs to prioritize the roads for investment. The MOT and the local governments should jointly profile the republican and local roads to facilitate the government's prioritization. The collected road profile information could be integrated into the RAMS database. It is suggested that the government determine minimum level of services for roads in the areas, identify gaps between existing conditions of roads and newly defined service levels, and translate the gaps into criteria for the said prioritization. The prioritization among roads in remote areas should correspond to the said national spatial development program for supporting their region's economic development.

138.   **Heighten attention to road safety and climate resilience in designing roads.** The road accident rate in Tajikistan is higher than that in the neighboring countries. Accidents can be prevented through behavioral change

and integration of road safety aspects in the engineering design. ADB-financed projects[62] have several ongoing initiatives related to road safety, such as developing guidelines on safe road design and improving black spots on selected national highways. The guidelines are under the MOT's review for adoption, while the improvement of selected black spots is ongoing. Such initiatives would help the MOT accumulate practical knowledge on road safety and disseminate it among its staff and relevant enterprises/institutes. The accumulated knowledge should be institutionalized for the future evolvement of road safety initiatives. Proper monitoring and reporting of road accidents and their causes through database management is recommended to formulate future road safety initiatives in an evidence-based manner. Such an approach would be aligned with the current international movement as a response to the criticality of road safety.[63] In addition to road safety, accommodating climate adaptation designs in transport infrastructure is urgent to help safeguard road assets against any climate-related extreme events such as high seasonal precipitations, avalanches, and landslides, to make roads passable throughout the year. In this regard, cost-efficient and state-of-the-art technologies should be studied for immediate application.

139.   **Revitalize the railway subsector.** Tajikistan Railways' profits have been maintained, which is considered to be an outcome of deferring maintenance of existing infrastructure. The maintenance strategy currently placed would not reflect the maintenance needs of each infrastructure, resulting in lowering operational speed and service quality (para. 81). Given that the railway subsector is key for facilitating international trade, the reform of the subsector should be further examined, including the subsector restructuring. It should be noted that the previous commercialization and privatization of the railway subsector was not successful. The sale of Tajikistan Railways' multimodal terminals has resulted in price increases for the use of these terminals. The sale of spur lines to private companies caused additional needs for coordination with and payment to these companies whenever the spur lines need to be used to gain access. In addition to such extra transactions, Tajikistan Railways still needs investments in the existing infrastructure. Other reform options may be considered.

140.   One possible reform option would be the vertical separation of infrastructure ownership from railway operations. This option would call for all infrastructure, including spur lines and multimodal terminals, to be consolidated into a single government entity tasked with their maintenance using public funds. The other option would be giving railway companies such as Tajikistan Railways the license to operate train services on the infrastructure for a fee. Pursuing the commercialization of Tajikistan Railways as an OJSC is also an option, as discussed in detail in the Railway Sector Assessment (2021) (footnote 50). Detailed discussions will be needed to determine the railway subsector's strategic role for the country's growth and firm up the subsector's reform strategy accordingly.

141.   **Review financial viability and operational efficiency of aviation subsector operations.** The assessment pointed to unconstructive competition among airports. Such competition has adversely affected traffic demand, service quality, and financial or operational efficiency at each airport. Additionally, another competition is with the existing roads and railways, as air transport remains too expensive for people's regular use and those modes often serve as alternatives to air transport . The government should review and redefine the functions of each airport in the country's context. The restructuring of airport functions may eventually attract international airlines interested in operating flights to Tajikistan and/or forming alliances with local operators.

---

[62]   ADB. 2016. *Report and Recommendation of the President to the Board of Directors: Proposed Loan, Grant, and Administration of Grant to the Republic of Tajikistan for the Central Asia Regional Economic Cooperation Corridors 2, 5, and 6 (Dushanbe–Kurgonteppa) Road Project.* Manila; ADB. 2018. *Report and Recommendation of the President to the Board of Directors: Proposed Grant to the Republic of Tajikistan for the Central Asia Regional Economic Cooperation Corridors 2, 5, and 6 (Dushanbe–Kurgonteppa) Road Project (Additional Financing).* Manila

[63]   The Asia Pacific Road Safety Observatory was established in February 2020 by several international development agencies including the ADB as the regional forum in the Asia and Pacific region on road safety data, policies, and practices, while the CAREC program facilitates high-level discussions among the CAREC member countries to implement actions stated in the Regional Road Safety Strategy for the countries (footnote 40). Both initiatives emphasize the importance of establishing the reliable road accident database.

142.   The interview with the CAA unveiled that the agency plans to invest in building additional airports and expanding or renovating infrastructure in the existing airports. The investment should be carefully examined because the number of air travelers will likely remain suppressed due to the COVID-19 pandemic. It will take time to return to the level before the pandemic. In 2020, Tajikistan closed the international airports for months to control the infection. The number of migrant workers from Tajikistan has subsequently reduced, following the recent shrinkage of job markets in the Russian Federation (footnote 16), as evidenced by the estimated drop of remittances by $1 billion.[64] It is recommended to carry out careful demand forecasts and assess potential impacts of the new investments to the existing airports. The decision about airport investments should be made in line with the suggested national spatial development program.

143.   In the meantime, air transport is still an option to improve domestic connectivity within the country, through such measures as expanding the domestic airports and introducing regular domestic flights to routes other than the route between Khujand and Dushanbe.

144.   **Improve the transport network's performance to facilitate international trade.** BCPs and logistic centers are considered an integral part of roads or railways infrastructure, and should be integrated into those infrastructure's development for strengthening the country's trade network and economic connectivity with the surrounding countries. For that, the strategic functions of each BCP or logistic center must be well defined for development when formulating the future transport sector program. To enable those facilities to perform their expected functions, the government should examine each facility's technical requirements as well as the applicability of state-of-the-art technologies to accommodate the modern needs of users from and to the surrounding countries. This examination would contribute to the improvement of the country's logistics performance.

---

[64]   ADB. 2020. *Tajikistan: Validation of the Country Partnership Strategy Final Review, 2016–2020.* Manila.

Appendix 1
Major Projects by Development Partners (Approved during 2000–2020)

Years	Project Name	Major Interventions	Development Partner	Loan/Grant Amount at Approval ($ million)
2020–2026	Fourth Phase of the Central Asia Regional Links Program	Rehabilitation of Bekabad (Uzbekistan Border)–Kurkat, Dehmoy–Ghafurov, Ghafurov–Kistevarz, and Kuchkak–Konibodom	World Bank	131.0 (grant)
2020–2024	Road Network Sustainability Project	Rehabilitation of Hulbuk–Kangurt and Okmazor–Dangara	ADB	67.5 (grant)
2019–2024	CAREC Corridors 2, 3, and 5 (Obigarm–Nurobod) Road Project	Construction of a new bypass on the Obigarm–Nurobod section	ADB EBRD OFID	110.0 (grant) 150.0 (loan) 40.0 (loan)
2019–2023	Project for the Rehabilitation of Kizilkala–Bokhtar Section of Dushanbe–Bokhtar Road	Rehabilitation of IR09 Kyzylkala–Bokhtar	JICA	30.7 (grant)
2019–2021	Tajikistan Air Navigation	Modernization of air navigation monitoring and control systems	EBRD	7.0 (loan)
2018–2023	CAREC Corridors 2, 5, and 6 (Dushanbe–Kurgonteppa) Road Project (Additional Financing)	Rehabilitation of IR09 Chashmasoron–Kyzylkala (40 km)	ADB	90.0 (grant)
2018–2023	Construction of Kulob–Kalaikhum Highway	IR04 Kulob–Sh. Shokhin IR04 Shkev–Kalaikhum (58 km)	IDB SFD KFAED OFID ADFD	14.0 (loan) 30.0 (loan) 25.5 (loan) 10.0 (loan) 15.0 (loan)
2017–2023	Strengthening Critical Infrastructure Against Natural Hazards Project	Rehabilitation of 18 bridges in GBAO region, and procurement of road maintenance equipment for GUSADs	World Bank	11.0 (loan) 8.0 (grant)
2017–2020	Project for Capacity Development for Road Disaster Management	Capacity building for the MOT's regional road administrations	JICA	3.2 (grant)
2016–2021	CAREC Corridors 2, 5, and 6 (Dushanbe–Kurgonteppa) Road Project	Rehabilitation of IR09 Dushanbe–Chashmasoron (33 km)	ADB OFID	49.4 (loan) 17.8 (grant) 12.0 (loan)
2016–2021	Dushanbe–Uzbekistan Border Road Improvement Project	Improvement of IR02 Dushanbe–Tursunzoda (5 km)	EBRD AIIB	62.5 (loan) 27.5 (loan)
2016–2019	Project for Improvement of Equipment for Road Maintenance in Sughd Region and the Eastern Part of Khatlon Region	Procurement of road maintenance equipment for GUSADs	JICA	16.5 (grant)
2016–2018	Project for Improvement of Air Navigation Services in Tajikistan	Training of Tajik Air Navigation	JICA	2.9 (grant)
2015–2020	Second Phase of Central Asia Road Links Program	Rehabilitation of Konibodom–Patar, Kuchkak–Guliston, and Dehmoi–Madaniyat (70 km in total)	World Bank	38.2 (loan) 6.8 (grant)

(continued on next page)

(Appendix 1 continued)

Years	Project Name	Major Interventions	Development Partner	Loan/Grant Amount at Approval ($ million)
2015–2019	Equipment for Road Maintenance	Procurement of road maintenance equipment for the MOT	EBRD	2.5 (loan) 2.5 (grant)
2015–2018	Project for Improvement of Dushanbe International Airport and its Phase 2	Cargo terminal, Instrument Landing System, Precision Alert Lighting System	JICA	18.1 (grant) 3.3 (grant)
2015–2016	Bridges and Tunnels on Vakhdat–Yovon Railway	Improvement of 5 bridges (712 m) and 3 tunnels (3,755 m)	Export-Import Bank of China	72.0 (loan)
2013–2020	CAREC Corridors 3 and 5 Enhancement Project	Rehabilitation of IR07 Sayron–Karamyk (88 km) and RR32 Vose–Khovaling (87 km)	ADB	70.0 (grant)
2013–2017	Reconstruction and Technical Re-Equipment of Khujand Airport	Rehabilitation of runways, installation of high intensity lights, and modernization of radio and ground control safety equipment	EBRD	3.9 (loan)
2013–2015	Project for Improvement of Equipment for Road Maintenance in Khatlon Region and Districts of Republican Subordination	Procurement of road maintenance equipment for GUSADs	JICA	16.8 (grant)
2013–2014	Dushanbe–Kulma Highway Rehabilitation	Improvement of RR026 Dangara–Kangurt (24 km)	PRC	26.8 (loan)
2012–2017	Construction of Kulob–Kalaikhum Highway	IR04 Kulob–Kalaikhum (40 km)	IDB SFD KFAED ADFD OFID	20.0 (loan) 20.0 (loan) 17.0 (loan) 15.0 (loan) 13.0 (loan)
2012–2017	CAREC Corridor 6 (Ayni–Uzbekistan Border Road) Improvement Project	Rehabilitation of IR13 Ayni–Uzbekistan (113 km)	ADB OFID	100.0 (grant) 14.0 (loan)
2012–2014	Construction of Dushanbe Airport Terminal	Dushanbe international terminal	France	26.5 (loan)
2011–2016	CAREC Corridor 3 (Dushanbe–Uzbekistan Border) Improvement Project	Rehabilitation of IR02 Dushanbe–Tursunzoda–Uzbekistan Border (67 km)	ADB	120.0 (grant)
2011–2014	Shagon–Zigar Road Rehabilitation Project, Phase 3	Rehabilitation of IR04 Shagon–Zigar (18.8 km)	IDB	18.6 (loan)
2011–2013	Construction of Bridge in Shurobod District of Khatlon Region	Construction of bridge in Shurobod District of Khatlon Region	AKF	3.5 (grant)
2009–2014	Dushanbe–Kulma Highway Rehabilitation	Rehabilitation of IR04 Dushanbe–Dangara (136 km) Chormagzak/Khatlon Tunnel (4,450 m)	PRC	243.4 (loan)
2007–2010	Road Maintenance Development Project	Procurement of 100 pieces of equipment for GUSADs	EBRD	4.0 (loan)
2007–2013	CAREC Regional Road Corridor Improvement Project	Rehabilitation of IR07 Dushanbe–Karamyk (121 km) and 8 bridges (715 m)	ADB	40.9 (loan) 12.5 (grant)
2007–2010	Shagon–Zigar Road Rehabilitation Project, Phase 2	Rehabilitation of IR04 Shagon–Zigar (9.7 km)	IDB	13.8 (loan)
2006–2013	Dushanbe–Chanak Road Rehabilitation	Rehabilitation of IR01 Dushanbe–Khujand–Chanak (336 km) and Dusti and Shahristan tunnels (6,300 m)	PRC	281.1 (loan)
2006–2013	Project for Rehabilitation of Kurgan Tyube–Dusti Road	Rehabilitation of IR09 Bokhtar–Dusti (42 km and 18 km)	JICA JICA	33.7 (grant) 23.7 (grant)
2006–2010	Project for the Improvement of Dusti–Nizhniy Pyanzh Road	Rehabilitation of IR09 Dusti–Nizhny Panj (12.0 km and 15.4 km)	JICA	5.1 (grant) 19.1 (grant)

(continued on next page)

(Appendix 1 continued)

Years	Project Name	Major Interventions	Development Partner	Loan/Grant Amount at Approval ($ million)
2006–2009	Construction of Shar–Shar Tunnel	IR02 Shar-Shar/Ozodi Tunnel (2,250 m)	PRC	32.9 (grant)
2005–2013	Dushanbe–Kyrgyz Border Road Rehabilitation Project, Phase 2 and Additional Financing	Rehabilitation of IR07 Dushanbe–Karamyk (100 km) 15 bridges	ADB OFID	30.0 (loan) 20.0 (grant) 3.5 (loan)
2005–2010	Community-Based Rural Roads Maintenance Project	Maintenance works provided to selected rural roads	ADB	1.8 (grant)
2005–2007	Construction of Bridge over Pyandzh River (Tajikistan–Afghanistan)	IR09 Bridge at Panji Poyon	US	28.0 (grant)
2003–2015	Istiklol Tunnel Construction	IR01 Istiklol/Anzob Tunnel (5,000 m)	IRN	5.0 (grant) 21.2 (loan) 16.0 (grant)
2003–2010	Bridge Construction	Bridges in 4 districts of Gorno Badakhshan Autonomous Region	AKF	4.3 (grant)
2003–2008	Dushanbe–Kyrgyz Border Road Rehabilitation Project, Phase 1	Rehabilitation of IR07 Dushanbe–Karamyk (89 km) and selected rural roads, totaling 77.7 km	ADB OFID	15.0 (loan) 6.0 (loan)
2003–2005	Shkev–Zigar Road Rehabilitation Project	Rehabilitation of IR04 Shkev–Zigar (37.8 km)	KFAED OFID SFD	16.3 (loan) 4.0 (loan) 6.0 (loan)
2001–2005	Shagon–Zigar Road Rehabilitation Project, Phase 1	Rehabilitation of IR04 Shagon–Zigar (5.5 km)	IDB	9.1 (loan)
2000–2007	Road Rehabilitation Project	Rehabilitation of IR04 and IR10 Dushanbe–Kulob (80.0 km, selected road section only) Rural roads totaling 150 km	ADB OFID	20.0 (loan) 4.0 (loan)
2000–2002	Construction of Murghab–Kulma Road Project	IR04 Murgob–Kulma (32.6 km)	IDB	9.7 (loan)

ADB = Asian Development Bank, ADFD = Abu Dhabi Fund for Development, AIIB = Asian Infrastructure Investment Bank, AKF = Aga Khan Foundation, CAREC = Central Asia Regional Economic Cooperation, EBRD = European Bank for Reconstruction and Development, GBAO = Gorno–Badakhshan Autonomous Oblast, GUSAD = Government Automobile Road Establishment, IDB = Islamic Development Bank, IR = international road, IRN = Islamic Republic of Iran, JICA = Japan International Cooperation Agency, KFAED = Kuwait Fund for Arab Economic Development, km = kilometer, m = meter, MOT = Ministry of Transport, OFID = OPEC Fund for International Development, PRC = People's Republic of China, RR = republican road, SFD = Saudi Fund for Development, US = United States.

Note: Bokhtar was formerly known as Kurgonteppa, and the updates were made only in the column of "Major interventions." Some sector programs were not included due to the limited information.

Source: Asian Development Bank.

Appendix 2
Republican Roads in State Register

Code	Name	Length (km)
RR 001	Hushyori–Khoja Obi Garm Resort	5.70
RR 002	Anzob passway–Khoja Sangkhok Spring	12.10
RR 003	Rugund–Khavotag Resort	10.10
RR 004	Pugus–Takob–Safedorak	18.30
RR 005	Varzob Hydropower System–Kharangon–Dusti Camping	10.90
RR 006	Shahrinav Town–Cheptura Railway Station (from 42 km of IR 02)	6.00
RR 007	Shahrinav Town–Karatogh Resort	3.40
RR 008	Shahrinav Town–Karatogh Village	4.50
RR 009	TALCO Plant–Tursunzoda Town	3.10
RR 010	School # 59 of Hissor–Hissor Town	3.00
RR 011	Langar–Almosy Village	12.20
RR 012	Tula–Shohambari Village	8.30
RR 013	Kalenin–Tursunzoda Town	2.80
RR 014	Yangishahar–Yangimazor–Tandykul (Jirgatol District)	22.00
RR 015	Chanor–Darband Bypass	4.20
RR 016	Sari Pul–Navobod	18.20
RR 017	Khoit 1–Nazarayloq Coal Mining Deposit	41.00
RR 018	Zankon–Jirgatol Village	4.00
RR 019	Karamyk–Jirgatol Village	2.00
RR 020	Chailagan–Lakhsh Airport	1.60
RR 021	Nimij–Sayron (from Khoit side)	35.00
RR 022	Vakhdat–Romit	37.00
RR 023	Chormaghzak–Khuchaloni Village	4.40
RR 024	Chormaghzak–Yovon (Bypass Road)	23.00
RR 025	Chashma–Norak Town	5.30
RR 026	Dangara–Kangurt–Baljuvon–Khovaling	70.40
RR 027	Somonchi–Olimtoi Khurd	9.80
RR 028	Komsomol–Shaftolubogh–Tajikistan–Somonchi	29.20
RR 029	Guliston–Mir Said Ali Hamadoni District Center	13.10
RR 030	Qurbonshahid–Temurmalik	31.80
RR 031	Temurmalik–Kangurt	27.00
RR 032	Vose–Khovaling	87.70
RR 033	Kulob–Muminobod	41.80
RR 034	Ziraki–Dahana (Kulob Town)	6.80
RR 035	Kulob–Airport	3.50
RR 036	Tugarak–Sarichashma–Chagam–Shuraobod	47.50
RR 037	Kalaikhum–Dashti Luch Airport	6.90
RR 038	Surkhsangov–Dursher (via Vanj District Center)	61.30
RR 039	Barchid–"Vakhdat" Town–Pakhor	4.60
RR 040	Andarob–Garmchashma Resort	6.20
RR 041	Khorug–Roshtkala–Tukuzbuloq	154.50
RR 042	Dushanbe–Rudaki–Lohur Interchange	11.60
RR 043	Rudaki–Yovon–Abdurahmoni Jomi–Uyaly	107.00
RR 044	Chimteppa–Hissor	20.00

(continued on next page)

(Appendix 2 continued)

Code	Name	Length (km)
RR 045	Lohur–Esamboy–Sayod	80.90
RR 046	Lohur Interchange	2.10
RR 047	Norak Hydropower Plant Terminal–Karabuloq	9.90
RR 048	Dushanbe–Ayni Village–Hissor	16.10
RR 049	Rossiya Farming Center–Guliston Farming Center (Rudaki District)	9.10
RR 050	Joint Stock Company Uljaboy–Qiblai Farming Center (Rudaki District)	23.90
RR 051	Abdurahmoni Jomi–Kyzylkala	13.50
RR 052	Road to Closed Joint Stock Company Kimiyo of Tajikistan–Cyprus Joint Venture	4.50
RR 053	The turn to 201 Military Division Base–Temporary Parking to Tunnel of Norak Hydropower Plant	12.00
RR 054	Bokhtar–Vakhsh	13.80
RR 055	Sabzavot–Railway Station Bokhtar	0.90
RR 056	Obshoron Street of Sarband Town–Sarband Town	2.00
RR 057	Vakhsh–Danghara	50.00
RR 058	Uzun–Jilikul–"Tigrovaya Balka" National Park	32.50
RR 059	Jilikul–Garavuti	9.20
RR 060	Dusti–Jilikul	5.70
RR 061	Jaloliddin Rumi–Jilikul	10.40
RR 062	Komsomol–Pakhtakor	8.40
RR 063	Ruknobod–Shurcha–Rudaki Mausoleum	17.00
RR 064	Gagarin Street of Istaravshan–Ghonchi	12.60
RR 065	Dairy factory–Istaravshan Town	4.20
RR 066	(Istaravshan) District Center Approach Road	16.40
RR 067	Zafarobod–Bekobod Town–Uzbekistan Border	34.20
RR 068	Yova–Khujand	17.30
RR 069	Konibodom–Noorafshon–Isfara	27.00
RR 070	Konibodom–Ravot–Uzbekistan Border	14.00
RR 071	Qahramon–Chilmahram	11.00
RR 072	Road to Khujand through Okteppa Village	7.00
RR 073	Ovchi–Qalacha	13.60
RR 074	Ayni District–Mastchohi Kuhi	55.00
RR 075	Stalinobod–Khujand Airport	2.20
RR 076	Somgar–Adrasmon Village	33.00
RR 077	Shahriston District Center Approach Road	5.00
RR 078	Isfara–Shurob Village	7.00
RR 079	Degmoy–Jabbor Rasulov District Center	6.20
RR 080	Yakkatol Village Approach Road	1.20
RR 081	Khushekat–Firdavsi	14.20
RR 082	Ghalaba–Konibodom Railway Station	7.10
RR 083	Konibodom Railway Station–Konibodom Resort	4.00
RR 084	Qahramon–Shaydon Town	11.30
RR 085	Rushan–Basid–Savnob	150.00
RR 086	Maykhura–Takfon	62.00
RR 087	Ergash–Sangtuda Hydropower Plant	18.00
RR 088	Isoev village–Guliston Village–Vakhsh Village	41.60
RR 089	Kadiob–Roghun Town	10.75
RR 090	Khujand–Palos	16.60
RR 091	Kurkat–Bekobod–Uzbekistan Border	11.60
RR 092	Sari Pul–Miyonadu Sovkhoz	36.00
RR 093	Fayzobod–Fayzobod District Center	1.70
RR 094	Kabudchar–Sicharogh–Aligalabon	10.34
RR 095	Khovaling–Siyofark–Shugnov	63.00
RR 096	Binokor–Chashma–Bahor	12.00
RR 097	Zardolu–Chormaghzak–Nayzirak	24.39
RR 098	Bahor Main Street of Kurghontepa (Bokhtar)–Hoji Sharif Market	4.90

IR = international road, km = kilometer, RR = republican road.

Source: Decree No. 625 on Names and Indexes of Highways of Republican Significance, dated 30 October 2015.

Appendix 3
Regional Road Administrations and Government Automobile Road Establishments

Unit	Total Roads (km)	International/ Republican Roads (km)	Local Roads (km)	Staff (no.)
Hissor Regional Road Administration				**26**
GUSAD Vakhdat	352.5	111.6	240.9	54
GUSAD Varzob	226.0	134.0	92.0	41
GUSAD Rudaki	326.1	174.6	151.5	53
GUSAD Shahrinav	94.5	24.9	69.6	24
GUSAD Hissor	246.6	70.2	176.4	33
GUSAD Tursunzoda	283.4	28.7	254.7	30
GUSAD Fayzobod	186.5	49.7	136.8	31
GUSAD Norak	128.0	61.7	66.3	31
GUSAD Roghun	72.4	25.0	47.4	25
Total Hissor Region	**1,916.0**	**680.4**	**1,235.6**	**348**
Kulob Regional Road Administration				**27**
GUSAD Danghara	334.3	107.4	226.9	61
GUSAD Kulob	223.4	44.1	179.3	43
GUSAD Baljuvon	69.5	42.5	27.0	27
GUSAD Vose	275.4	109.0	166.4	48
GUSAD Hamadoni	209.7	26.1	183.6	42
GUSAD Farkhor	411.2	95.4	315.8	70
GUSAD Temurmalik	213.8	48.9	164.9	41
GUSAD Muminobod	169.2	26.0	143.2	33
GUSAD Khovaling	226.4	110.7	115.7	32
GUSAD Shamisiddin Shohin	228.2	91.0	137.2	43
GUSAD Yakhchipun	82.5	46.5	36.0	27
Total Kulob Region	**2,443.6**	**747.6**	**1,696.0**	**494**
GBAO Regional Road Administration				**26**
GUSAD Saghirdasht	116.0	36.0	80.0	24
GUSAD Darvoz	245.8	172.3	73.5	58
GUSAD Vanj	254.1	101.3	152.8	49
GUSAD Rushon	182.5	125.5	57.0	53
GUSAD Barntang	278.0	118.0	160.0	40
GUSAD Murgob	641.1	388.6	252.5	97
GUSAD Ishkoshim	439.9	294.9	145.0	80
GUSAD Shughnon	137.1	79.8	57.3	43
GUSAD Ghund	233.5	189.0	44.5	69
GUSAD Roshtqala	200.4	154.5	45.9	45
Total GBAO Region	**2,728.4**	**1,659.9**	**1,068.5**	**584**
Rasht Regional Road Administration				**23**
GUSAD Nurobod	156.1	65.1	91.0	40
GUSAD Rasht	198.8	68.7	130.1	42
GUSAD Lakhsh	80.6	42.6	38.0	24
GUSAD Jirgatol	175.6	90.0	85.6	34
GUSAD Sangvor	101.4	101.4	0.0	30

(continued on next page)

(Appendix 3 continued)

Unit	Total Roads (km)	International/ Republican Roads (km)	Local Roads (km)	Staff (no.)
GUSAD Tojikobod	111.5	25.0	86.5	26
GUSAD Hoit	112.8	76.0	36.8	26
Total Rasht Region	**936.8**	**468.8**	**468.0**	**245**
Bokhtar Regional Road Administration				**25**
GUSAD Kushoniyon	231.9	53.5	178.4	35
GUSAD Panj	284.2	45.1	239.1	38
GUSAD Kubodiyon	178.5	34.5	144.0	34
GUSAD Abdurahmoni Jomi	227.6	45.5	182.1	36
GUSAD Jaloliddin Balkhi	250.7	70.0	180.7	36
GUSAD Vakhsh	236.8	67.4	169.4	37
GUSAD Levakand	111.8	58.3	53.5	34
GUSAD Noriri Khisrav	104.9	45.0	59.9	32
GUSAD Jayhoon	255.8	74.2	181.6	39
GUSAD Yovon	234.7	79.5	155.2	45
GUSAD Dusti	235.6	85.0	150.6	44
GUSAD Khuroson	264.8	73.0	191.8	45
GUSAD Shahrituz	133.4	38.7	94.7	42
Total Bokhtar Region	**2,750.7**	**769.7**	**1,981.0**	**522**
Sughd Regional Road Administration				**27**
GUSAD Ayni	350.0	237.2	112.8	65
GUSAD Bobojon Ghafurov	431.5	191.8	239.7	80
GUSAD Panjakent	296.9	82.7	214.2	67
GUSAD Devashtich	233.4	35.8	197.6	44
GUSAD Spitamen	198.3	33.8	164.5	35
GUSAD Konibodom	291.2	86.8	204.4	64
GUSAD Mastchoh	153.7	30.7	123.0	31
GUSAD Isfara	274.1	107.6	166.5	58
GUSAD Istaravshan	269.9	77.7	192.2	56
GUSAD Jabbor Rasulov	255.5	39.0	216.5	31
GUSAD Zafarobod	205.4	41.2	164.2	34
GUSAD Mastchohi Kuhi	151.0	0.0	151.0	29
GUSAD Shahriston	136.4	68.1	68.3	28
GUSAD Asht	316.3	116.3	200.0	53
Total Sughd Region	**3,563.6**	**1,148.7**	**2,414.9**	**702**
Grand Total	**14,339.1**	**5,475.1**	**8,864.0**	**2,895**

GBAO = Gorno-Badakhshan Autonomous Oblast, GUSAD = Government Automobile Road Establishment.

Source: Government of Tajikistan, Ministry of Transport.

References

Asian Development Bank (ADB). Project Preparation Technical Assistance for CAREC Corridors 2, 5, and 6 Road Project (Dushanbe–Kurgonteppa) (TA-8945). Technical Assistance Consultant's Report on Road Asset Management System. Unpublished.

ADB. Technical Assistance Consultant's Report: Country Governance Risk Assessment Tajikistan. Technical Assistance for Enhancing Governance and Capacity Development as Driver of Change (TA-9061). Unpublished.

ADB. 2000. *Report and Recommendation of the President to the Board of Directors: Proposed Loan and Technical Assistance Grant to the Republic of Tajikistan for the Road Rehabilitation Project.* Manila.

——. 2004. *Project Performance Audit Report for Postconflict Infrastructure Program in Tajikistan.* Manila.

——. 2013. *Report and Recommendation of the President to the Board of Directors on Proposed Loan and Grant to the Kyrgyz Republic and the Republic of Tajikistan for Central Asia Regional Economic Cooperation Regional Improvement of Border Services Project.* Manila.

——. 2016. *Country Partnership Strategy: Tajikistan, 2016–2020.* Manila.

——. 2017. *Safely Connected: A Regional Road Safety Strategy for CAREC Countries, 2017–2030.* Manila.

——. 2019. *Technical Assistance Consultant's Report: Road Asset Management Road Map.* Manila (TA-8789 REG: CAREC Knowledge Sharing and Services in Transport and Transport Facilitation).

——. 2020a. *Asian Development Outlook 2020 Update–Wellness in Worrying Times.* Manila.

——. 2020b. *CAREC Corridor Performance Measurement and Monitoring: Annual Report 2019.* Manila.

——. 2020c. *Key Indicators for Asia and the Pacific 2020.* Manila.

——. 2020d. *Strengthening Support for Labor Migration in Tajikistan: Assessment and Recommendations.* Manila.

——. 2020e. *Tajikistan: Validation of the Country Partnership Strategy Final Review, 2016–2020.* Manila.

——. 2021a. *Basic Statistics 2021.* Manila.

——. 2021b. *Railway Sector Assessment for Tajikistan.* Manila.

ADB and Central Asia Regional Economic Cooperation (CAREC). 2020. *CAREC Corridor Performance Measurement and Monitoring: Annual Report 2019.* Manila.

Deutsche Gesellschaft für Internationale Zusammenarbeit. 2020. *Climate Change Profile: Tajikistan*. Dushanbe.

Government of Tajikistan. 2011. *National Target Development Program for the Transport Sector of the Republic of Tajikistan up to 2025*. Dushanbe.

———. 2016. *National Development Strategy of the Republic of Tajikistan for the Period up to 2030*. Dushanbe.

———. 2020. *Road Asset Management System Program for 2021–2024*. Dushanbe.

Government of Tajikistan, Ministry of Economic Development and Trade. 2016. *Mid-Term Development Programme of the Republic of Tajikistan for 2016–2020*. Dushanbe.

International Monetary Fund. 1998. *Tajikistan: Recent Economic Developments*. IMF Staff Country Reports Vol. 1988/16. Washington, DC.

McMahon, K. and S. Dahdah. 2008. *The True Cost of Road Crashes: Valuing Life and the Cost of a Serious Injury*. Basingstoke: International Road Assessment Programme.

Observatory of Economic Complexity. Tajikistan. https://oec.world/en/profile/country/tjk (accessed 20 October 2021).

Statistics Agency under the President of the Republic of Tajikistan. 2019.

———. 2020. *Population of the Republic of Tajikistan as of 1 January 2020*. Dushanbe.

United Nations Environment Programme. 2015. Tajikistan Climate Facts and Policy: Policies and Processes. https://wedocs.unep.org/bitstream/handle/20.500.11822/9861/-Tajikistan_climate_facts_and_policy _policies_and_processes-2015country_scorecards_for_climate_policy_Tajikistan.pdf.pdf?sequence =3&isAllowed=y (accessed 20 October 2021).

World Bank. Logistics Performance Index (Country Score Card). https://lpi.worldbank.org/international/scorecard (accessed 20 October 2021).

———. 2013. *Tajikistan: Overview of Climate Change Activities*. Washington, DC.

———. 2015. *Project Appraisal Document on a Proposed Credit in the Amount of SDR 26.5 million (US$ 38.25million) and a Proposed Grant in the Amount of SDR 4.7million (US$ 6.75milllion equivalent) to the Republic of Tajikistan for the Second Phase (CARs-2) of the Central Asia Road Links (CARs) Program*. Washington, DC.

———. 2020a. *Guide for Road Safety Opportunities and Challenges: Low- and Middle-Income Country Profile*. Washington, DC.

———. 2020b. Poverty in Tajikistan 2020. Infographic. 15 October. https://www.worldbank.org/en/news/ infographic/2020/10/15/poverty-in-tajikistan-2020 (accessed 20 October 2021).

———. 2021. Assessment of Economic Impacts from Disasters Along Key Corridors. Washington, DC.

World Health Organization. 2018. *Global Status Report on Road Safety*. Geneva.

www.ingramcontent.com/pod-product-compliance
Lightning Source LLC
Chambersburg PA
CBHW042034220326
41599CB00045BA/7382